WARS THAT NEVER END

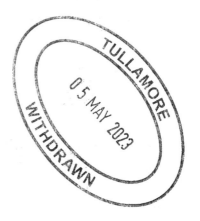

Published by Brolga Publishing Pty Ltd
ABN 46 063 962 443
PO Box 12544
A'Beckett St
Melbourne, VIC, 8006
Australia

email: markzocchi@brolgapublishing.com.au

National Library of Australia Cataloguing-in-Publication entry

Ferguson, Ian
Wars That Never End : The Horrific Impact of Post War Stress
9781922175823 (paperback)
Post-traumatic stress disorder.
War--Psychological aspects.
Combat--Psychological aspects.
616.85212

Printed in Australia
Cover design & typesetting by Wanissa Somsuphangsri

BE PUBLISHED

Publish through a successful publisher. National distribution, Macmillan
& International distribution to the United Kingdom, North America.
Sales Representation to South East Asia
Email: markzocchi@brolgapublishing.com.au

WARS THAT NEVER END

Ian Ferguson

DEDICATION

This book is dedicated to the thousands of service personnel and their associated families and loved ones, who have suffered physically and mentally from Australia's involvement in wars.

ACKNOWLEDGEMENTS

My heartfelt thanks to the many people who have helped *Wars That Never End* come to fruition.

Bill Gammage (AM), who is currently an Adjunct Professor and Senior Research Fellow at the Humanities Research Centre of the Australian National University, has generously allowed me to use many quotations from his fine book *The Broken Years*.

The Australian War Museum Library and Research Centre in Canberra, have also provided vital access to material which is especially relevant for the contents of this book.

I also thank Les Wight for the use of many of his extensive collection of war history books and magazines, and the many other people who have provided useful assistance for my research.

Some kindly agreed to be interviewed, and the information and insights they provided added greatly to the quality of the book. I am also grateful for receiving valued photographs from Marlene and Ian Day, Boz Parsons, George Cops, Ted Baulch, Ernie Brough, Mick Bergin and Frank McLennan.

As always, I am indebted to my wife Ann for her ongoing support, and I add a special note of thanks to Pat Ashe for proof reading my manuscript.

Ian Ferguson, April 2015

CONTENTS

CONTENTS

AUTHOR'S NOTES

"War is just idiotic... If all the politicians, and men over forty, were sent to war, there wouldn't be a war. They would sit down, have a beer, and find another way."

The pragmatic, common sense views expressed above, were contained in a book titled *Dangerous Days - A Digger's Great Escape*. It was written by Ernest J. (Ernie) Brough, and was published in 2009. Ernie is now aged 94. He is a World War II veteran, who was awarded a Military Medal, (MM), for displaying 'courage in persistent attempts to escape POW camps'.

History suggests that Ernie's optimistic solutions to end all wars have little chance of success. Aussie soldiers first fought overseas in 1885. Between then and 2015, Australia has had a military presence in various overseas locations for close to 70 of those 130 years. Furthermore, during that time our country was only under direct military threat for three years, when Japan was invading neighbouring countries in the Asia-Pacific region. Such information suggests that successive Australian governments, and the majority of voters, continue to initially support our international involvement in various armed conflicts.

Significantly, in September 2014, Australia committed itself to provide military assistance to America and other allies in Iraq and possibly Syria. In that area of the Middle East,

Islamic State (IS), (a fanatical group of Muslim militants), had become a perceived new threat to world peace.

Ernie's excellent book, along with other personal observations provided by approximately 50 war veterans and their families in interviews, diary entries and letters from various war fronts, are all vital sources of information for this book titled *Wars That Never End*. Editorial views of newspapers, the works of various other war history authors, and documents from the Australian War Museum and the ABC News website, were also used extensively.

Wars That Never End primarily examines the effects that modern warfare has on the lives of Australian families. My research findings suggest that most service personnel bring their war experiences home with them, in one form or another. Modern warfare is a life changing experience which some cope with adequately. Others struggle to adapt, and sadly some die from suicide, alcohol and other drugs of dependence, because of their unresolved wartime traumas.

On the AM radio program in November 2014, ABC journalist Chris Uhlmann revealed the staggering fact that the number of serving and former Australian soldiers who've committed suicide, is now triple the combat toll of 40 that was recorded in the recent war in Afghanistan.

In some case studies included in this book, strong evidence can be linked with the positive and negative scenarios which individuals face. On other occasions evidence is more circumstantial, so readers are invited to reach their own conclusions about the outcomes which occur.

The spirit of mateship is an essential factor for gaining positive morale within Australian service personnel groups. Consequently, the importance of friendship in combat zones and post-war life is another continuing theme in *Wars That Never End.*

A chapter is also devoted to Australia's involvement in air combat, which arguably became the main factor behind Germany's defeat in World War II. These intrepid airmen lived life on the edge in those pioneer days of flight warfare, and the many perilous missions they undertook continually challenged their mental and physical health.

Finally, I have discovered in my research that many acquaintances in our daily lives are either ex-service people or have family connections to others who have served Australia proudly in various military zones of the world. They are all an essential part of our combat history, their personal memories of war service remain strong, and I honour their contributions in the chapter which concludes this book.

Statistically alone, it is obvious that wars of last century, and global combats of more recent times, have been disastrous for Australia. A staggering 61,000 Australians perished in World War I, and 21 years later the toll of Aussie lives in World War II reached nearly 40,000.

Ernie Brough is absolutely correct: War is idiotic. However this fine humanitarian and gallant war hero provides a ray of hope for the future at the conclusion of his fascinating book, when he declares that

"Humans are capable of creating 'heaven on earth'. Live your heaven on earth today."

(Ian Ferguson April, 2015)

1
AUSTRALIAN BRITONS

When the 20th century dawned over Australia, most of the colonial population took pride in the description of being 'independent Australian Britons'.

Our second Prime Minister Alfred Deakin proudly described himself in those terms, and Sir George Houston Reid, (Australia's High Commissioner in London during 1913), linked this description with Australia's British Empire responsibilities when he declared that

"Ties of loyalty... bind the Empire, and defend the flag which has always defended her... the British flag is the last line of defence against all forms of lawless conquest. The British Empire is the only nation and coloniser that has shown the ability to govern with wisdom and benevolence..."

It seems the general public mostly supported the views of the establishment, as the majority of people were descendants of white British forebears. In Australia during the early years of the 20th century, sectarianism between the protestant majority and the Catholic minority was rife. God was almost certainly an Anglican; the strongest swear word

Alfred Deakin

one would expect to hear or read was 'd..n', and temperance attitudes were applauded by many in the community.

Fervent affinity with 'the mother country' surfaced strongly in 1885, after Britain's General Gordon was assassinated by rebels in the Sudan. A prominent New South Wales (NSW) newspaper described Gordon as being 'a figure of heroic proportions', and governing members from the youngest colony in the British Empire, agreed with the British general's illustrious reputation. The NSW government cabled London, and offered to bankroll a local contingent to assist the 'mother country' in the Sudan. This generous offer was readily accepted by Britain with the proviso that their own officer assumed command of any colonial forces.

There were minor pockets of resistance within Australia to this imperial skirmish. Editorials in *The Bulletin* ridiculed the contingent plan, a few people in working class Sydney suburbs protested about the fund, and some miners in rural areas opposed the financing of an Australian contingent force.

In general, the public enthusiastically supported the call

to arms. Hundreds of young Australians embarked on the long and arduous pilgrimage to that remote area of North Africa to join their 'British brothers' in combat.

The Australians' eager commitment proved to be an anti-climax. 'The paltry affair' virtually finished before they

General Gordon arrived at their destination, and only

three of the 'Australian Britons' received wounds in the minor altercation.

Fourteen years later, imperialism remained an unofficial religion among Anglo-Saxon Australians after the Boer War broke out in South Africa. Once more Britain gained almost unequivocal support among influential areas of the Australian colonies. Leading newspapers highlighted the concept that Aussies were part of 'the imperial family', and large numbers of volunteers again left our shores to fight alongside British forces.

In Sydney thousands cheered off a shipload of excited soldiers bound for South Africa. The atmosphere was euphoric, and one optimist predicted that **"This war will be a great picnic."**

Storm clouds hung over the city on that festive day, and they proved to be an ominous symbol for this optimistic claim. Unfortunately, in the harsh reality of the veldt battle fields, British generals tended to underestimate the skill and resilience of the South Africans, who fought tenaciously for their independence. The determined enemy soon had three major towns under siege, and they unexpectedly gained the upper hand in early conflicts.

Back in Australia, communities tended to slavishly honour the imperialist message. The central Victorian town of Inglewood still only supports a population of a little over 1,000 people. However the staggering total of 44 young locals from this small hamlet volunteered to serve Britain and the Empire in the Boer War. Three of them perished in the South African campaign, with Nurse Frances (Fanny) Hines becoming the first Australian woman to die in an active service situation.

Another Ingleburn volunteer, Private E.L. Tatchell, corresponded from the battle fields quite regularly with a brother in Bendigo. An extract from a letter, quoted below, reveals that Tatchell whole-heartedly supported Britain's imperialist motives.

".. all soldiers fighting for the Queen, (Victoria), and for the credit of England and Australia... So far as I can judge, the Boers are a contemptible lot, and I consider one hundred Britishers equal to a thousand of them."

Captain Neville House, Trooper John Bidsee, Lieutenant Guy Wylly, Private James Roger, Lieutenant Leslie Maygar and Lieutenant Frederick Bell were all honoured with Victoria Crosses, (VCs), during the Boer War. One wonders if the motives of these six brave soldiers mirrored the attitudes of Private Tatchell, as well as leading newspapers, and government leaders of the time.

The Victoria Cross originated in the 19th century, after a cross bearing Queen Victoria's name was instituted in

1856. It was allegedly crafted from bronze taken from a Crimean War cannon.

It remains the most prestigious military award for bravery. All ranks of service are eligible for a VC award, as are civilians serving under military command. The main criteria in the selection process is displaying valour in the face of the enemy.

Each of the six Australian VC recipients from the Boer War clearly deserved to be decorated, as they rescued comrades in need while under heavy enemy fire. Neville House, John Bidsee, Guy Wylly and Leslie Maygar all demonstrated unswerving loyalty to Britain and the Empire by then committing themselves to serve in World War I, which broke out 12 years after the Boer War ended.

In civilian life, Sir Neville House was a medical practitioner, and he also became very prominent in public life. He was twice Mayor of the NSW town of Orange, and in 1922 he won the Federal seat of Calare for the National Party. During his seven years stint of Parliamentary service Neville House held several ministerial portfolios.

No known problems emerged in the post-war lives of House, Bidsee and Wylly. Leslie Maygar was a highly respected and long- serving army officer before he was killed in World War I action (KIA) in North Africa, and Private Rogers lived until the age of 86, after overcoming serious wounds which were sustained at Gallipoli during the same war.

The death of Major L.C. ('Elsie') Maygar in this war is especially poignant, because this fine horseman was KIA when he participated in the now legendary 'last great cavalry charge in history'. Trooper Ion Llewellyn, ('Jack') Idriess, (OBE), who later became a prolific and influential Australian writer, witnessed this spectacular foray from the emu plumed horsemen. He described the action in stirring terms.

Ion Idriess

"**At a mile distant, their thundering hooves were stuttering thunder...they were an awe-inspiring sight, galloping through the red haze, the dying sun glinting on their bayonet points. Machine guns and rifle fire roared, but the Brigade galloped on, (though) horse after horse crashed...**

The last half-mile was a berserk gallop, with the Squadron in magnificent line - a heart throbbing sight, as they plunged up the slope...Then came a whirlwind of movement all over the field. A rush of troops poured for the opening in the gathering dark... mad, mad excitement - terrific explosions from down in the town. Beersheba had fallen."

Idriess was wounded at Beersheba and previously at Gallipoli, where he frequently acted as a spotter for William

Edward ('Billy') Sing, a renowned sniper, who may have killed nearly three hundred Turks with his Lee-Enfield 303 rifle. The Gallipoli terrain was ideal for a skilled sniper to be effective, and none were more accurate with deadly attacks than this diminutive Asian-Australian from

North Queensland.

Sing became a controversial war hero. Some dubbed him 'The Assassin', while others described Sing as 'the Anzac Angel of Death'. In *Gallipoli Sniper: The Life of Billy Sing,* renowned author John Hamilton, bluntly describes Sing as being a 'cold blooded killer'. During 2010 a TV mini-series titled *The Legend of Billy Sing* was produced.

Billy Sing

Sing was wounded several times, both at Gallipoli and later on the Western Front. His marriage to a Scottish woman was short-lived, and during World War II Billy Sing died in poor circumstances in Brisbane. It seems safe to assume that Sing's wartime experiences had adverse effects on his post-war life.

It also appears clear that Ion Idriess, and the five Boer War VC recipients already profiled, were largely motivated by imperialist sentiments when they volunteered for war service. There is also no conclusive evidence that they suffered significant mental stress from their battlefield involvements. However, in regard to the final Boer War VC recipient, the opportunity for adventure may have been a more telling incentive than the call of

Lieutenant Frederick Bell

11

God, Queen and country.

Lieutenant Frederick William Bell from Perth was an adventurous man who lived an eventful life. After hostilities ceased on the veldt, he remained in Africa for much of his young adult years. At first he was an Assistant District Officer

in British Somaliland, where he was seriously injured after being mauled by a lion.

He rose to the rank of Captain after volunteering again for the Great War, and when that major conflict ended, Fred Bell became a District Commissioner in Kenya. At the age of 47 Bell married a widow, and following her death 22 years

Andrew "Banjo" Paterson

later, he married another widow. Fred Bell VC was living in England when he passed away at the age of 79.

Patriotic fervour at home marginally waned as the Boer War unexpectedly dragged on. Andrew Barton ('Banjo') Paterson, in his role as war correspondent for the *Sydney Morning Herald* and *Melbourne Age*, became one of the first journalists to criticise British war tactics.

Paterson, who later became a legendary Australian poet and writer, observed war action in South Africa for nine months, and during that time his initial support for British imperialism began to wane. Banjo became disillusioned about the lack of respect some incompetent British officers displayed towards Australian soldiers, and he also developed a grudging respect for the Boer's stubborn resistance.

Never-the-less, support for Britain's involvement remained strong in the Empire's youngest colony, until news about the execution of two Australian soldiers shocked many.

Harry ('Breaker') Morant was one Australian whose life ended at the hands of a British army firing squad. Following his controversial death, the womanising larrikin became a Ned Kelly type hero to many of his countrymen. Today Morant's name

Harry "Breaker"
Morant

is still more readily recognised, than any VC winners from the Boer War.

Like Fred Bell, it was probably a restless opportunity for adventure, which first enticed Harry Morant to volunteer for war service in South Africa. Exiting Australia quickly also allowed Breaker the opportunity to avoid debt collectors, as well as the many women he had betrayed.

Previously, during the 1870s in North Queensland, Harry Morant gained fame for his horse breaking skills, which gained him the nickname of 'Breaker'. He departed for South Africa on 26th January 1900, and Lance-Corporal Morant's riding prowess soon saw him become a despatch rider for London's *Daily Telegraph*. Around that time, Breaker also became engaged to the sister of Captain Frederick Hunt, an army friend he met during their shared action on the veldt.

The pair became aligned with a unit called the 'Bushveldt Carabineers', but on 5th August 1901, Hunt was killed during a fierce encounter with local Boers. One of the captives was later found to be wearing Hunt's uniform, an offence which the British commander, previously declared would result in a death sentence being imposed.

Nine Afrikaaners allegedly involved were executed by the Carabineers, and five members of that group were subsequently arrested by British officers. Morant, Peter Handcock and George Whitton were the Australians charged, and two British soldiers faced court martial proceedings for the same offence.

All five were found guilty of unlawful executions at a Pietersburg trial, but the punishments varied greatly. A defiant Morant and Handcock both received death sentences. George Whitton was later released after serving a custodial sentence of 28 months, while the two British offenders only received dishonourable discharges. Lord Kitchener signed the death sentence authorisations, and both Morant and Handcock were executed by a British firing squad.

Many Australians felt outraged and betrayed when news of the executions finally became public. The recently formed Australian Government demanded an explanation from Lord Kitchener, and aspects of the trial were criticised. Court proceedings had illegally been conducted in secret, and when the trials ended vital court room transcripts could not be found.

Lord Kitchener

Kitchener later visited Australia on a 'good will' visit, but he faced a potentially hostile situation when he opened a Boer War memorial in the NSW town of Bathurst. Peter Handcock's young widow and her three fatherless children resided in the area, and threats of public harassment were made. When the memorial was unveiled by the British military leader, the name of Peter Handcock was missing from the list of Bathurst Boer War casualties. Later, after Kitchener departed, his name was added to the roll call of locals who had died for Britain and the Empire.

Over a century has passed since the Boer War ended, but Breaker Morant still enjoys more celebrity status than any other past Boer War veterans. In 1980 Bruce Beresford directed a blockbuster movie titled *Breaker Morant*, with Edward Woodward playing the leading role, while Bryan Brown portrayed Handcock. Since 2010 former Australian navy lawyer, Jim Unkles, has unsuccessfully sought to gain a posthumous pardon for Morant.

Such interesting developments are of secondary importance, compared to the fact that a significant change occurred in sentiments about the Empire in 'the land down under'. British authorities executed two Australians, but inflicted only 'a slap on the wrist' to British subjects found guilty of the same crime. This perceived injustice produced a 'hair-line fracture' in the trust the two countries had with each other, and became a source of future friction.

The final pre-Gallipoli war action became known as the Boxer Rebellion, which occurred in China between 1900 and 1901. Once more Australian volunteers rallied to the cause of British imperialism, but it was a low key skirmish. There were six Australian fatalities from the uprising, but these deaths were all illness related.

2

WARTIME HONEYMOON CONTINUES

In the first decade of the 20th century, tensions between European countries further strengthened Australia's strong relationship with Britain. A final flashpoint for armed conflict in Europe occurred at Sarajevo on 28th June 1914, when Serbian nationalists assassinated Archduke Ferdinand and Duchess Sophie, who were the heirs to the Austro-Hungarian Empire. Their murders set off a chain of events, which ended with Britain declaring war on Germany.

By then Australia was only 13 years into nationhood, and both Prime Ministers of that era had been born in Britain, as had most Australians of the time. Automatically, as a British Empire country, Australia was at war with Germany once Britain made its solemn declaration, and the overall response was enthusiastically supportive across our fledging nation.

"...The British fleet is our all in all. Its destruction means Australia's destruction, the ruin of our trade, and the surrender of our liberties," asserted the *Melbourne Punch*.

"The British Empire is our family circle, and we cannot live outside it."

This adamant editorial was typical of newspaper support for Australian involvement in the Great War. Media enthusiasm extended across most of the country, with the

Andrew Fisher

Sydney Morning Herald declaring our involvement would be 'a baptism of fire'.

Church and community leaders were also vocal in their public support, and strong bi-partisan support was evident from the major political parties of the time. At a public rally on 31st July 1914, Andrew Fisher, (the soon to be elected Prime Minister), famously declared that **"Australians will stand beside their own, to help defend her, ('the mother country'), to our last man and our last shilling."**

Incumbent Prime Minister Joseph Cook then offered to place Australian vessels under complete control of the British Admiralty. Cook also predicted that thousands of recruits would immediately volunteer for active service with British forces.

Such rash promises from the nation's leaders produced a rush of eager candidates to recruiting stations. Private Charles Bingham later expressed the motivations of many volunteers, in an interview with historian Harvey Broadbent.

Joseph Cook

"It was a feeling that England was the mother country... it was (also) a feeling that 'this is your duty'. That's why I think the majority enlisted."

Other interviewees cited the lure of adventure, and the security of a regular pay packet, as being prime motivational influences for 'joining up'.

An overall sense of euphoria swept the nation, and many small communities mirrored the example of Inglewood in Central Victoria during the Boer War.

Laidley, which lies 70 kilometres west of Brisbane, still only has an approximate population of 3,500 residents, but 500-600 local men volunteered for World War I service.

However, despite such examples of local enthusiasm, the growing toll of casualties began to impact negatively on the general public, and the number of able bodied men who answered the call fell short of the ever growing total of recruits who were required. At the time, Australia registered a population of 4.95 million people, and by the end of 1914, only 53,000 males had signed up from the 820,000 men who fell within the age range of availability.

Consequently, official recruitment campaigns became assertively personal. The message below, from a brochure of that time, reveals how determined government bodies became in their recruitment tactics.

5 Questions to Men Who Have NOT ENLISTED!!!

- If you are physically fit, and between 18 and 44 years, are you really satisfied with what you are doing today?
- Do you feel quite happy, as you walk along the street and see OTHER men wearing a King's uniform?
- What will you say in years to come, when people ask you "Where did YOU serve in the Great War?
- What will you answer, in years to come, when your children grow up and say "Father! Why weren't you a soldier too?
- What would happen to the Empire if everyone stayed at home?

Aggressive division was evident within a few local communities. White feathers, (symbolising cowardice), were sometimes left in the letter boxes of households where unenlisted males lived. Young women were encouraged to reject courtship overtures from males who did not heed the call for wartime action.

N.G Ellsworth, who was then a Melbourne Mint official, took that possible threat seriously, and confided in a letter that **"If I had stayed at home, I would never have been able to hold my head up, and look any decent girl in the face."**

Unfortunately, Ellsworth's romantic inclinations were short lived. He was only 31 when he died from war wounds in 1917.

By October 1914, Germans were portrayed as being evil and barbarous, which resulted in some Australian families of Germanic origin being economically and socially ostracised.

Your King and Country
Need You.
ENLIST TODAY!

E.H. Chinner, a bank clerk from Peterborough in South Australia before enlisting, was noticeably paranoid in his attitude to the enemy.

"...Very keen to get to grips with those infamous brutes... to do something to wipe out such an infamous nation...I am sure that God will take a strong hand in the war and punish Germany."

Chinner was thwarted in his wish to humble the German

enemy. In 1916 the 22-year-old Lieutenant died from his wounds in a POW camp.

Overall, nothing destroyed the euphoria which gripped much of the pre-World War I Australian population. On 4th August 1914, when Britain declared war on Germany, enthusiastic crowds sang 'God Save the King' on the streets, bands played 'Rule Britannia' in cafes and theatres, and Melbourne's town hall was decked out in the empirical colours of red, white and blue.

During the four-year course of the war, more than a million socks were knitted for troops, and many paper boys reportedly donated money earned from their daily rounds. By the end of 1916 Victorian students had raised over £145,000 for their war relief efforts, and those who enlisted displayed similar enthusiasm. Some allegedly rode, walked or sailed hundreds of miles to recruitment stations. Eighteen-year-old Victorian R.E. Antill, who was then an apprentice cabinet maker, confided to his parents by letter that

"...I am itching to get a dig at a few Germans... we have all got war fever... I am too excited to give my mind to writing tonight..."

Tragically, this young man enjoyed very few more sleeps, as three years later he was KIA.

A.J. McSparrow, a Parramatta railway employee prior to the start of World War I, informed his parents that

"I have enlisted... and I don't regret it in the very least. I believe that it is every young fellows duty...We are the sort of men who should go."

Young McSparrow's idealism also ended prematurely. He was only 26 when he died from war wounds in 1917.

3

RELATIONSHIP PROBLEMS EMERGE

"They went with songs to the battle,
They were young, straight of limb,
True of eye, steady and aglow…"

(Laurence Binyon)

Between August and September 1914, the Australian government began their war preparations. By the end of October, 26 Australian and New Zealand warships were docked in the deep waters of Albany's King George Sound in Western Australia.

On November 1st the first of Australia's excited volunteer servicemen began their long voyage to training camps in the Middle East. Morale of the war novices was boosted en route near the Cocos Islands, when members of the fleet sank the German Raider vessel 'Emden'. No doubt a few jubilant songs were sung by the Anzacs on their way to the far off battle.

Disappointingly, after the Australian and New Zealand Corps (ANZACs) arrived in Egypt, the first few weeks of training became a monotonous anti-climax. The majority of the Diggers were bachelors aged between 20 and 34. They often resented the parade type discipline which the majority of British officers favoured, and many stand-off situations developed between the two groups.

The Aussies had travelled half-way around the world to fight for God, King and Empire, and they felt deflated when they were 'dumped in this land of sin, sand, shit and syphilis'.

Overall, their training camps based in the searing heat of the Egyptian desert had little relevance to the formidable mission which lay ahead in a far different environment.

Corporal R.E. Antill complained that

"The sand and hot weather is killing us… the sooner (we are) out of this place and in the firing line the better…soon we will round the Dardanelles, or the south of France, and then the fun will start."

The local traders in the Cairo markets also wished the visiting soldiers were elsewhere, as the Aussie Diggers frequently caused mayhem with their brawling, vandalism and whoring in seamy areas of the city. Recent statistics reveal that as many as 60,000 Australian troops contracted some form of venereal disease during World War I. This health issue represented a major problem for military authorities, who desperately needed fit and healthy combatants for future war zones.

Relief for all involved in Egypt came in December 1914, after the British General Staff in London formulated a plan, which author Peter Cochrane later described as being a 'gambler's dream'.

Britain decided to force a sea and land passage through the Dardanelles, a strategy which would secure the Suez Canal and provide easy access to invade the Turkish capital of Constantinople, (now Istanbul). In his book, *Australians at War,* Cochrane described the overall plan as one that 'aimed for maximum results with minimum investment'. It was the Anzac forces in Egypt who were assigned to undertake this 'mission impossible'.

On 4thApril 1915, they sailed from Alexandria to the Dardanelles. Feelings then expressed by the soldiers in letters to their families, friends and loved ones displayed a range of emotions, as they neared their moment of destiny.

"If we go down, you can rely that we've done our best for King and country," declared Captain H.E.S. Armitage, an Adelaide school teacher who was KIA less than two years later.

Sergeant M.J. Ranford, a Boer War veteran from Semaphore in South Australia, was more circumspect in a tender letter penned to his wife Gladys.

"We are about to take part in some very severe fighting, and there is no doubt that those who come through it alive, will be very lucky. If I should go under, there is no need for me to say of who my last thoughts will be…"

The 35-year-old ganger survived the Gallipoli landing, but perished on the battlefields of Europe four months later.

Unfortunately, the hastily prepared invasion strategy never went to plan. The Diggers believed they would land on an open plain, and little resistance was expected from the Turkish defenders. In actuality, the first Brigade landed about a kilometre from the intended starting point. Lance-Corporal George Mitchell, an adventurous Adelaide clerk who became a highly decorated officer by the war's end, was approximately 100 yards from the beach south of Ari Burnu, when the first bullets shattered the stillness. Later, Mitchell made this defiant diary response.

Lance Corporal
George Mitchell

"...Wee-wee-wee, came the little messengers of death. Then it opened up into a terrific chorus...The key was being turned into the lock of hell...Some laughed and joked...Fear was not at home."

Over 600 men died at Anzac Cove in the first landing, so the casualty rate for just one battle was 100 more than for the entire Boer War. From the steep cliffs above, Turkish marksmen decimated the first onslaught of Anzac troops, and a more subdued George Mitchell later recorded his thoughts about the mayhem he had witnessed.

"'Fix bayonets and prepare to charge,' came an order... I think about one man in six was capable of advancing, the others were all dead or wounded... no man could live erect in that tornado for many seconds."

Over 2,000 Anzacs were either killed or badly wounded during the first three days of the Gallipoli invasion, and the gruesome statistics continued to escalate during the brutal Dardanelles campaign. More than 2,300 Australians were killed or wounded at Lone Pine, and when an emotional roll call was conducted after the ill-fated battle at the Nek, only 47 of the original 550 Light Horse Brigade were present to confirm their names. Officially, during the short Gallipoli campaign, 8,709 Australian lives were lost and 1,944 received injuries.

Sergeant Archie Barwick, who was formerly a Tasmanian farmer, was consistent in his strong support for the imperial cause in his Gallipoli diary entries. However, after witnessing the carnage at Lone Pine, even he had momentary doubts about the conduct of the war.

"I had a terrible fight with myself... one part of me wanted to run away and leave the rest of my mates to face it."

Today, legends associated with service in Gallipoli seem even more compelling to the increasing number of Aussies who make the 'pilgrimage' to the Dardanelles.

The 25th of April 2015 marked the 100th anniversary of Anzac Day. The Australian Government allocated millions of dollars to effectively 'market' this momentous occasion and strictly controlled the number of visitors who attended the centenary service at the historic Turkish venue.

"Honour the dead, our country's fighting brave,
Honour our children left in foreign graves,
Where poppies blow and sorrow seeds her flowers,
Honour the crosses marked forever ours."
(Extract from *Honour the Dead* - words written by Shirley Erena Murray, music composed by Colin Gibson)

Battle sites evoked intensely personal responses among many old and young visitors. As Les Carlyon notes in his compelling book titled *Gallipoli*

"(It) is a place of the mind: everyone who goes there sees it the way they want."

Most Australian households in 1915 had a direct or indirect link to World War I casualties and, to some, the war never ended. Today the graveyard tributes found in this now peaceful area of Turkey, often reflect the values of that era. The messages express both grief and imperialistic pride, and are still inextricably linked to the first Anzacs.

"A Place is Vacant in Our Home which can Never be Filled."

This heart-rending message is carved on the headstone of Private H. Andrews. He was 46 when he was KIA on 15th November 1915.

"Only a Boy, But Died as a Man for Liberty and Freedom."

The parents of 18-year-old Private H.J. Burton left this lasting tribute. He died in action on 30th November 1915.

"Gave up His life for His King and Country," was the homage paid to 28 year-old Peter A. Smith, while Bombardier W.H. Benson received the following accolade on his headstone.

"The Supreme Sacrifice for God, His King and Country."

During the actual campaign, the combination of multiple deaths, poor diet, flies, maggots, disease, insomnia and inadequate medical facilities, disillusioned even the most hardened and optimistic men on the front line. While fighting for his life on 400 Plateau, a more philosophical George Mitchell then viewed death

"…not as the welcome risk of glory, but as the painful shutting out of all life's promise."

R.E. Antill, who strongly supported the war cause initially, was now much more circumspect, in the views he states below.

"I must honestly say I will be highly delighted when this war is over, for it is simply terrible to see your pals shot down beside you...(it)is enough to drive a fellow mad...I tried to get a couple of hours rest, (but) I had to use a dead man's legs for a pillow."

However, for home readers, Australian newspapers were inclined to downplay examples of rampant carnage, and they tended to glamorise horrific battle-front incidents. Ellis Ashley-Bartlett and other celebrity war correspondents, noted 'fallen' rather than 'dead' soldiers in their columns, and those killed were honoured for 'paying the supreme sacrifice'. Defeats were redefined as 'good progress skirmishes', and an ever growing list of 'gallant' officers were paid fulsome homage.

While fatalities on the battle-front escalated, tensions between the British high command and the Aussie Diggers continued to simmer. The casual attitudes Australians exhibited towards authority infuriated English officers, while the Australians' respect for their officers' decision making continued to plummet.

Major Garret Adcock, who was formerly a mining engineer from the Victorian wine-growing area of Rutherglen, consistently demonstrated his loyalty for the imperial cause throughout the war. This competent soldier, however, became disillusioned with many British officers he observed. Adcock provided the following blunt comments.

"The British bungling has sickened me...all overseas troops have had enough of the English. How I wish we were with our own people instead of under the English all the time."

Incompetent leadership was clearly a major factor in the

huge casualty rate at Gallipoli. Belatedly, after the debacle experienced at the Nek, General Sir Ian Standish Monteith Hamilton, (then Commander of the Mediterranean Allies Expeditionary Force), was recalled to London. Never-the-less other dangerously incompetent officers were retained, and in some cases even promoted, despite their legacy of ongoing failures. A callous disregard for human life often characterised their decision making.

General Sir Alymer
Hunter-Weston

"Casualties? What do I care for casualties?" barked General Sir Alymer Hunter-Weston after receiving information about the growing death toll. Little wonder the luckless Anzacs under his command dubbed Hunter-Weston 'the butcher of Helles'. He was later surprisingly elevated to the rank of Corps Commander.

Les Carlyon, the highly respected Australian writer, who was awarded an Order of Australia (AC) in June 2014 for his 'dedication to words', is scathing about Hunter-Weston's war service legacy. Carlyon also criticises Sir Alexander Godfrey and Sir Frederick Stoppford for their gross incompetence. The common strategy for such officers was to oversee bayonet charges against heavily fortified Turkish trenches in daylight hours. Furthermore, when these tactics inevitably failed, Plan B would be a repeat of that same strategy a day later.

The Australian officer, Lieutenant-Colonel John ('Bull') Antill, was also criticised by Carlyon for his major role in facilitating the mass slaughter at the Nek. Inexplicably, after Antill resigned from army service in 1924, he was named an honorary Major-General.

Overall, the cracks which vaguely threatened relationships between England and Australia at the end of the Boer War, widened noticeably by the time Anzac soldiers withdrew from Gallipoli.

Lieutenant Colonel
John Antill

4

WORLD WAR 1 CASE STUDY: THE TRAGIC LIFE OF HUGO ('JIM') THROSSELL (VC)

"There's a lonely stretch of hillocks
There's a beach asleep and drear…
There are sunken, trampled graves,
There are lines of buried bones…
There's unpaid waiting debt,
There's the sound of gentle sobbing in the south."

(Extracts of a 1916 poem written at Gallipoli, by Sergeant Leon Gellert of the 10th Battalion)

In his early years, Hugo ('Jim') Throssell enjoyed all the privileges available to those born into the landed gentry. The handsome and likeable young man was a lauded public figure after becoming Western Australia's first VC recipient. However Throssell's life began to change dramatically after he fell in love with a woman who later became a foundation member of the Australian Communist Party.

A besotted Jim Throssell publicly shunned the values of his upbringing. He was ostracised by many influential people, debts began to mount, and his life fell apart. The war hero was only 49 when he committed suicide.

To what extent did Jim Throssell's war experiences influence the tragic final outcome which ended his life?

Hugo Vivian Hope Throssell was born in Northam Western Australia, on 26th October 1884. He was one of 14 children, and George and Anne Throssell followed a family tradition when they provided somewhat exotic birth names for their children, but used more conventional titles in everyday life. Consequently Hugo was commonly called 'Jim', while Frank Erick Cotterell Throssell, (Jim's favourite brother), was always referred to as 'Ric'. Ric Throssell was two years older than Jim, and the pair remained close friends until death separated them. Jim later named his only son after the deceased Ric.

Their father was a 'self-made' man. George Throssell originally purchased a small grocery/post office store in Northam, which soon became a thriving business that serviced the Kalgoorlie goldfields. Judicious property purchases also assisted George Throssell to accumulate considerable wealth. He was dubbed 'the lion of Northam',

he became a parliamentarian in a conservative Western Australian government for seven years, and he also served as state Premier over a three-month period.

In summary, George Throssell was a wealthy and influential man who held abstemious and pious values. No work was allowed on his property on Sundays, and the presence of vice-regal guests at his sometimes lavish home dinners still

George Throssell

resulted in no alcoholic drinks being served. Jim Throssell reportedly consumed alcohol for the first time in Gallipoli when he swallowed a small amount of whiskey on the eve of the now infamous battle at Hill 60.

Jim Throssell was 11 years of age when Ric and he became boarding students at Adelaide's Prince Alfred College. At school Jim was a popular champion athlete, and he frequently stayed at the homes of nearby South Australian friends during long school holidays.

Sometime after Jim's school days ended, Ric and he purchased a small farm at Cowcowing. It was an arduous experience. Living conditions were primitive and the remote and arid property suffered terrible droughts. The advent of World War I was possibly a godsend for the struggling Throssell brothers. Their mother had died in 1906, their father passed away four years later, their inheritance fell short of what might have been expected, and neither Ric nor Jim had impressive employment credentials.

Regular pay packets of six shillings a day beckoned from the army, imperialism was a strong force in their culture, and the opportunity for travel and adventure was probably attractive. By early October 1914, the bachelor brothers left their Cowcowing property in the hands of a neighbour, and enlisted in the army.

They were placed in the Western Australian based 10th Light Horse Brigade, which began its training program at Perth's Royal Agricultural Showgrounds.

Jim Throssell was commissioned as a 2nd Lieutenant, and both Ric and he travelled to Egypt with the Brigade. There, much to his frustration, Jim was left behind to care for the regiment's horses, when most of the 10th Light Horse

Brigade was shipped to Gallipoli.

At that stage of his life Hugo Vivian Hope Throssell was 26 years-of age, and there were no obvious signs of mental deterioration in his behaviour.

Jim finally joined his army mates on 4th August 1915, three days before the infamous Nek battle erupted. The 10th Brigade suffered horrendous losses in that 'FOOL charge' (Jim's description). Eighty-two men were killed within minutes by the Turks, before his group was fortunately withdrawn from the needless carnage. Jim then reportedly became more motivated to engage the enemy in hand-to-hand combat. His opportunity came between 29th and 30th August 1915 at Hill 60, where heavy losses of life had already occurred.

New Zealand Trooper James Watson, who was attached to the Auckland Mounted Rifles, penned the following brief summary of the battle, which starkly highlighted the grim futility of the Anzac's task.

"We gained about 400 yards on four days fighting. One thousand men were killed or wounded."

Major Allanson was more graphic in his descriptions about the horrendous scenes on Hill 60.

"The whole place is strewn with bodies... the smells, (another of the major horrors of war), is appalling, the sights, disgusting and revolting. Our work is so heavy we cannot add to it by burying the bodies."

In this unnerving environment, Lieutenant Throssell became an inspiration to his troops. He killed five Turks in hand to hand combat after his group gained control of a trench. Later the enemy launched a fierce counter attack. Though seriously wounded, Throssell refused to leave his post or have his injuries addressed until imminent dangers had been overcome. During the night-long battle he allegedly hurled hundreds of small bombs into enemy territory, and constantly encouraged the men under his temporary command to fight on. Throssell must have been a fearsome sight, as his face was covered in blood for much of the action.

His heroic example produced the following accolade from an admiring fellow Light Horseman.

"He, (Throssell), wore no jacket, but had badges on the shoulder and straps of his shirt. The shirt was full of holes from pieces of bomb, and one of the broken badges had been driven into his shoulder."

After finally receiving treatment for his wounds, Lieutenant Throssell was transported to a London hospital for specialist treatment.

In October 1915 fate intervened while Jim was recuperating in hospital. At the time, a young, attractive and recently acclaimed Australian woman writer named Katharine Susannah Prichard was visiting the city. This newcomer to fashionable literary circles had become a celebrity, and a friend arranged a publicity photographic opportunity, which featured Katharine and the handsome young Australian hero recovering from war-time injuries. An instant attraction developed between Jim and Katharine, though they did not meet again for some time.

Lieutenant
Hugo Throssell VC

On 4th December 1915 Lieutenant Hugo Vivian Hope Throssell accepted an invitation to visit Buckingham Palace, where King George V awarded Victoria Crosses to Throssell and fellow Australian recipients William Symons, John Hamilton and Frederick Tubb. Jim Throssell's VC notification had arrived in mid-October when he was seriously ill in hospital. He had contracted bacterial meningitis while undergoing a routine operation.

Jim was the first Western Australian to be honoured with a VC. Much pride about this achievement was evident in his home state, while in London he was feted at various luncheons. Ominously however, this physically fit man was suffering from constant headaches and insomnia. When he returned home to Western Australia for the first anniversary of Anzac Day, he sometimes appeared to be nervy and confused. In one illuminating interview with a reporter, the usually reticent Jim made the following candid admission about the August 1915 action at Hill 60.

"It was horrible, ghastly. I have seen some horrible things."

The Medical Board obviously still harboured doubts about Jim returning to active duty, as they ordered a further three months of medical treatment and recuperation. During his convalescence, areas of rural Western Australia and Adelaide made much of their celebrity war hero at various functions, but Jim Throssell appeared to be overly nervous and shy in his public appearances.

Katharine Prichard

In late June 1916 Jim met up again with Katharine Prichard in Melbourne. A whirlwind romance developed between the strapping conservatively raised soldier from the landed gentry, and the radical socialist from middle class suburbia. Katharine privately came to believe, when the young couple shared an idyllic interlude at Emerald in the Dandenong Ranges, that

"Jimmy was broken by the war."

His continuing insomnia and nervous behaviour still allegedly troubled the Medical Board. Despite such reservations, Jim Throssell re-joined the 10th Light Horse Regiment for active service on 22nd January 1917. After initially training once more in Egypt, he was reunited again with brother Ric. The pair fought together in the World War I desert campaign.

There the mayhem of Gallipoli was tragically re-visited. Under the inept leadership of Britain's General Sir Archibald Murray, the 1st Battle of Gaza was a complete disaster. A second attempt to take Gaza was also doomed from the start, with eight soldiers from Jim's Regiment being killed. Jim was included among the 92 Diggers who were wounded.

Tragically, Ric Throssell was one of the fatalities. Jim allegedly issued secret whistle calls which the brothers had shared from their farming days, when he desperately attempted to locate and rescue Ric, but it was all in vain.

A devastated Jim Throssell spent much of his own three month recuperation grieving for Ric, which probably did little to improve his own mental health. Concerned colleagues noticed, after Jim returned to active duty, that the energetic Western Australian had lost much of his previous zest for action. After contracting malaria in the Jordan Valley, Jim Throssell was in and out of hospitals for the next six months of 1918. Thankfully he returned to Australia in October, where he re-united with Katharine.

The couple married in a Melbourne Registry Office on 28th January 1919, when Jim was 34 and Katharine 35. Jim was discharged from the army, and the couple purchased a property at Greenmount near Perth. The two soul-mates appeared to be very happy; probably happier than Jim had ever been.

He became employed as a soldiers' representative with the Returned Soldiers' Land settlement Board, and he also worked for the State Department of Agriculture. However, reckless borrowing from banks began a downward spiral in the Throssell's economic welfare.

Peace Day celebrations on 19th July 1919, (when the entire British Empire celebrated the signing of a peace treaty with Germany), became a crucial date in Jim Throssell's life. The mayor of Northam arranged for the town's most famous resident to lead a parade, and to be the guest speaker at a special banquet. One supportive local poet penned a tribute about the new town hero on a post card, which is now housed at the Australian War Museum Library in Canberra. A stanza from 'Fighting Jim' is shown below.

> **"It's a proud day for you, and prouder for us**
> **So do forgive us this bit of a fuss**
> **That we're making of you,**
> **Northam's own H.V.T.**
> **And added to that a well-earned VC."**

The editorial which appeared in the *West Australian* expressed similar sentiments, and described Jim Throssell as being

"A splendid specimen of the Australian race."

On that day in Northam, an estimated crowd of 1,500 people gathered to hear Hugo Throssell's address. Members of Jim's family were among the group of mostly conservative farmers, but the speech Jim made was completely at odds with their entrenched values.

"This war has made me a socialist...it has made me think what the causes of war...are," announced Jim to his shocked audience.

He then spoke passionately against all wars, capitalism, the profit motive, and he lauded the merits of communist type collective farms being established across the nation. Jim's family was embarrassed, while most of the crowd felt betrayed by his revolutionary speech.

In later years, Jim's son Ric stated that Katharine was the driving force behind her husband's controversial address. Naively, it appears that the couple expected the speech to be well received, but the 'Queensland Worker' was one of the few newspapers which supported his views.

The speech led to Jim and Katharine being socially shunned and politically side-lined. Community outrage then escalated more when Katharine Throssell became a foundation member of the Australian Communist Party. After she gave birth to Ric in 1922, she made the new baby a gown which had a hammer, sickle and an ear of wheat embroidered on the garment.

Soon after the 1919 Peace Day debacle, the Northam branch of the Returned Soldiers League, (RSL) urged the state Premier to remove Captain Throssell from his position with the Land Settlement Board, and he was never invited to speak again at a war commemoration gathering. It was not until 28th August 1999 that a memorial for Hugo Throssell was unveiled in Northam, and his memorial was far more modest than most tributes erected for other Australian VC winners.

In summary, the combination of his brother's death, his divisive marriage, the ill-conceived speech, and, above all, the cumulative effects of many harrowing war experiences, mentally tipped Jim Throssell 'over the edge'. His behaviour became even more erratic and unpredictable, and various mad-cap ventures ended in financial disaster.

In the early 1930s Jim Throssell unsuccessfully searched for gold. Later, shortly before his death, while Katharine, (with Jim's approval), was visiting Russia, he ambitiously attempted to establish a rodeo at their Greenmount property.

Fine weather attracted a crowd of over 2,000 people to the Sunday opening. However Jim was unable to benefit financially from his lavish business venture, as Western Australian laws of the time forbade the collection of entrance money for events staged on Sundays.

By then poor physical and mental health had noticeably aged the now fragile warrior, who faced the daunting prospect of financial ruin. By September his son Ric was being mostly cared for by friends, and Hugo Throssell had virtually become a recluse.

By mid-November 1933 a depressed Jim Throssell believed he had ruined everything of worth, and dreaded Katharine's reactions when she returned. He penned this last despairing note.

"I can't sleep, and I feel my old war head. It's gone 'phut', and that's no good for anyone concerned."

George Withers, a concerned brother-in-law, was then staying with Hugo at the Greenmount home. When he walked out on the veranda on the morning of 19th November 1933, he found Hugo Throssell's body. The tortured war hero had shot himself in the temple early that morning, and his suicide note was found nearby.

At Hugo's funeral, the presiding chaplain had no doubts about the cause of his death.

"He died for his country, as surely as if he had perished in the trenches," the celebrant informed the mourners.

Katharine's travel arrangements were delayed, and she arrived back in Australia about a month after the funeral. Katharine Throssell was 85 when she died in 1969.

Ric Throssell became a career diplomat, but believed the stigma of his mother's communist beliefs never left his life. He also committed suicide, on the same day that his terminally ill second wife passed away.

Various issues covered in this chapter shaped the course of Hugo Throssell's life, but horrific war experiences appeared to be the biggest single contributor behind his tragic death.

5

OTHER HAUNTED AND INTREPID WAR VETERANS

"...Hell let loose. It was fearful yet awe-inspiring. Some fellows' nerves gave way, and they became gibbering idiots – sergeants and all sorts... Fighting here is simply a massacre."

This description was provided by Corporal Arthur Thomas, a former manager of a tailoring firm, from the Melbourne suburb of Toorak. The English-born Thomas was a 40 year-old married man with a family, when he was KIA on the Western Front on 16th September 1918.

Thomas' graphic description captures the essence of that which Hugo Throssell endured, both on Hill 60 and later in Gaza. Little wonder that his 'nerves gave way'.

A countless number of war veterans have struggled to shake off the mental demons that haunt their lives after serving on front line battle fields. One tragic example was Private Martin O'Meara.

Martin O'Meara was an Irish born soldier, who was involved in fierce fighting when he served as a stretcher bearer with the 16th Battalion on the Western Front in World War I.

At Pozieres in France, between 9th and 12th August 1916, Private O'Meara rescued numerous wounded soldiers from 'no-man's land' during four days of fierce fighting. He also

Private Martin
O'Meara VC

provided precious supplies of food, water, ammunition and bombs to trenches that were under siege. Martin O'Meara's incredible bravery was rewarded with a Victoria Cross.

Physically, a wounded O'Meara survived the war and returned to Western Australia. Mentally, he was completely wrecked.

O'Meara spent most of the rest of his life in the Claremont Mental Hospital, where he was considered to be uncontrollable. Between the hours of 4.30 p.m. and 11 a.m., Martin O'Meara had to be kept under restraint in a straitjacket. This dreadful daily routine lasted for 16 years, until the poor lost soul mercifully died at the age of 50.

*

Wilfred Collinson

"I never conceived that war could be so dreadful... the whole place was spread with the dead... the sight of the limbs, the mangled bodies and the stray heads I saw with my own eyes... (it) sent a score of men go raving mad." (Diary entry from Lieutenant John Raws, who was a journalist in his pre-war days)

Wilfred Collinson spent the final 35 years of his life at the Bundoora Repatriation Mental Hospital. There this slightly built white haired old man would sit in his wicker chair, smoking endless numbers of roll-your-own cigarettes and chatting to himself.

Previously the 19 year-old from Yorkshire had only been in Australia for a few months before he enlisted in the army in 1914. In May of the following year, he was constantly under heavy fire at Gallipoli. He then served as a gunner on the Western Front for two years, and during that awful ordeal he was gassed three times.

Initially, after World War I ended, Will Collinson settled well into civilian life. He married his neighbour Carline, helped raise their four children, and was employed as an engineer at the Newport rail yards in Melbourne. However, by the mid-1930s, Will's lung and arthritic problems grew worse. Sleep became increasingly difficult and his mood changes were abrupt and aggressive.

In 1936 Collinson was committed to Mont Park Psychiatric Hospital, from where he was transferred permanently to Bundoora.

Every Saturday then became a pilgrimage for his wife. She would commute from her Canterbury home to Bundoora, first by train, horse and cart, and later by train and bus, until she died in 1954. Her children and grandchildren then took over visiting responsibilities, until a 77-year-old Will Collinson passed away in 1972.

"Two stretcher bearers found us in a shell hole; my mate was dead, and myself nearly frozen to death... our boys and 'Fitz' lay huddled together as they fell... It makes me shudder now to think of it." (Private Michael Ryan's Western Front observations in 1917)

*

Private Edward
John Ryan

Private Edward John Ryan, VC, was a World War I hero, whose life was also ruined by war traumas. On 30th September 1918, Ryan's 55th Battalion was involved in dangerous action near Bullecourt in France. When his group attacked a German post, Private Ryan was among the first to reach their defences. His fearless combat skills enabled the Battalion to overcome the enemy forces, and Ryan was again well to the fore, when the Germans launched a fierce counter attack.

Ryan led a group in a bayonet and bombing charge, which accounted for three Germans. The 28-year-old native of Tumut in NSW received a shoulder wound in the skirmish, but his valour enabled his Battalion to capture a trench, and disperse the remainder of the enemy.

Sadly, after returning to civilian life, 'Smiling Johnny' Ryan did not adapt well to peacetime society. He became a heavy drinker, who occasionally performed labouring tasks as he drifted around the country. The slightly built little man was virtually a vagrant when he died in Melbourne at the age of 51.

John Ryan was buried with full military honours at the Springvale Crematorium.

"Adieu, the years are like a broken song.
And the right grow weak in the strife with wrong.
The lilies of love have a crimson stain

And the old days will never come again."

(Diary entry of an anonymous Australian soldier,
written in September 1917)

Private Bruce Steel Kingsbury and Private Alan Avery enjoyed a life-long friendship which first began in a Melbourne primary school. The two later worked together as itinerant labourers in various parts of NSW and Victoria, before serving together as World War II soldier mates with the 2/3rd Pioneer Battalion in New Guinea.

There, on 29th August 1945, in the year the war ended, Bruce Kingsbury's incredible bravery earned him a posthumous VC.

On that fateful afternoon at Isurava, Kingsbury's platoon had been virtually decimated by the Japanese. Private Kingsbury volunteered to counter-attack the enemy when it appeared likely that the Australian's defences would soon be broken.

Firing his Bren gun from the hip, and screaming defiant abuse as he advanced, Kingsbury rushed down a hill towards the enemy, cutting a swathe through their ranks in his manic charge. He accounted for approximately 30 enemy soldiers during his reckless attack. Surviving Digger mates never forgot Kingsbury's instinctively brave act, when enemy bullets almost seemed to bounce off him.

Many followed his example, and added their own withering fire as they advanced.

Private Bruce
Kingsbury VC

Then, just as the courageous hero appeared to have survived, a lone Japanese marksman stood up and fired a single shot at Kingsbury, who was reloading his Bren gun.

The gallant Aussie slumped to the ground, and it was Private Alan Avery who rushed Kingsbury back to the Regimental First Aid Camp. There Dr Don Duffy gently informed Avery that his best mate had been killed, and the hero's friend was inconsolable.

"Just three minutes ago, he was so full of life,
Firing his Bren from his hip.
When all of a sudden he's hit
And my best mate falls
'Tell them I tried', he said,
And my words of good-bye
Froze on my lips."

(*What Do You Say to a Dying Man?*
- A tribute poem by Sergeant Bede Tongs, 3rd Battalion)

Sadly, on-going grief marred the rest of Alan Avery's life. After returning to civilian life he became a heavy drinker, and his marriage collapsed. The restless nurseryman's health suffered, and a move to Queensland did not solve his problems. War memories continued to haunt him, and in May 1997 Alan Avery shot himself dead.

Suicide among war veterans is not uncommon. Another World War II Digger reportedly committed suicide on the very day he was discharged. On 16th March 2013, *Melbourne Herald Sun* journalists, Ruth Lamperd and Patrick Carlyon, revealed more recent alarming statistics.

In their newspaper profile they claimed that in Brisbane

alone, (since Christmas 2012), 11 ex-soldiers had suicided, after serving in locations such as Rwanda, East Timor, Iraq and Afghanistan. During that same period of time, two Victorians, one Western Australian and another war veteran from NSW, also took their own lives.

This disturbing trend continues to escalate. On Tuesday 7th April 2015, the ABC reported that at least six junior sailors based at HMAS Stirling base in Western Australia had killed themselves over a two year period.

Forty-one Australian servicemen paid the supreme sacrifice in the Afghanistan War. However it is reliably estimated that three times this number have killed themselves since returning to civilian life, while hundreds more cope poorly with combat nightmares which continually reoccur. As many as 3,000 of these veterans are currently homeless, problems with alcohol are widespread, domestic violence is prevalent, and relationship breakdowns are common.

Former Army General John Cantwell recently warned that there is now a 'tsunami' of such cases. Mark Binskill, the current Chief of the Defence Force, believes Cantwell's claim is exaggerated, but he also admits that mental health problems among war service personnel are often ongoing and continuing to rise.

"It could be that it presents itself when they get out... (even) 15 or 20 years later."

In the past, 'shell-shocked' described mental disorders caused by war traumas. Today those affected are said to be suffering from Post-Traumatic Stress Disorder, (PTSD).

This condition may develop after a person is exposed to one or more traumatic events. Symptoms include disturbing and recurring flashbacks of memory, an avoidance of, or a numbing reaction to a specific problem, and hypo-active reactions to memory cues about the disturbing event.

If any or all of the above continue a month or more after the distressing experiences occurred, it is most likely that a PTSD reaction is being experienced.

This condition currently affects men more than women and children, and war veterans are most commonly at risk. One study concludes that 20% of all veterans who participated in military action in Iraq or Afghanistan will suffer some form of PTSD.

Early detection of the condition is beneficial, though it will not necessarily cure a developing problem. Debriefing opportunities are advantageous, (as soon as possible after the stressful incident has occurred), and such sessions usually include individual and group psychotherapy interviews. This procedure allows the individual to directly confront potential problems early, and assists in establishing a meaningful reconstruction of the traumatic event.

Some prescribed medications are valuable for treating the condition, especially when they are taken shortly after the confronting situation ends. Healthy and supportive relationships, regular exercise, and ongoing physical interests also assist the rehabilitation process.

On 9th March 2015, television journalist Quentin McDermott presented a compelling ABC *Four Corners* program which highlighted the distressing outcomes that many Australian war veterans experience, after returning from tours of duty in Afghanistan.

Jamie Tanner is one who constantly battles his past combat demons. He still suffers 'melt downs' when he withdraws from human contact, and does not communicate with family members for days on end. In one distressing recent incident he nearly assaulted his stepson after 'freaking out' in a crowded queue. This former section commander now acknowledges that his promising military career has prematurely ended.

Many other war warriors find it difficult to regain their grip on normality. Matthew Tonkin witnessed horrific scenes in the muddy combat fields of Afghanistan. One close mate lost both his legs, he saw dead comrades wrapped in blood stained blankets, and another mate was murdered by an Afghani colleague in a 'green on blue' attack. Matthew Tonkin struggled to readjust to the more mundane world of civilian life, and he died from a drug overdose in July 2014. In regard to PTSD problems for war veterans, his grieving father believes "**The worst is still to come.**"

*

OTHER PTSD CASE STUDIES

(Some information on the following four PTSD case studies was researched from *The Battle After War*, an article written by Kumi Taguchi.

His well-researched article was presented on the ABC News website in September 2014).

*

Before 'the incident' occurred, 'David' was determined to achieve two major goals. He aimed to rise up through the ranks in the Air Force, and he wanted to retire at 55. One milestone was partly achieved after David became a sergeant, but his second target has now been abandoned.

By October 2014 he was due to be discharged prematurely at the age of 50, and it remains unlikely that he will ever be capable of gaining employment of any kind.

"I was ten foot tall, bulletproof, nothing could get in the way of what I wanted to achieve," he recalled wistfully.

Previously in 2004, when David was undertaking his second stint in the Air Force, 'an incident' completely changed the course of his comfortable and predictable life. He feels unable to share any details of that past trauma which now haunts his daily life. However the trigger for his sudden breakdown was only the mundane sound of a car hitting a metal object behind him. This trivial moment brought ghastly past war memories flooding back into his life.

"Suddenly I was lying on the ground crying, I was a mess."

Now he's confined to a Melbourne hospital room for an indefinite period of time, because his life began to leak like a rusty pipe. Once his self-esteem started to seep away, it just wouldn't stop. At first David did nothing, while the quality of his life gradually flowed away. Long lasting bouts of anger became habitual, he was frequently depressed, and he felt disconnected from his wife and children. Finally his desperate partner gave him the following blunt warning.

"If you keep talking to me like a piece of shit, I'll leave."

Soon after the shocked David undertook a 12 week outpatient PTSD program, from where he's 'graduated' to Ward 17 of Melbourne's Heidelberg Repatriation Hospital. His companions are other current and former servicemen and women, who have also hit 'rock bottom'.

David is now being proactively treated for PTSD, but his greatest fear currently remains unanswered:

Will he ever be right again?

*

'Tim' was once 'Mr Perfect'. He enlisted at the age of 17, and his progress towards specialised work in the infantry was rapid. He took pride in his appearance, he was confident socially, and his future appeared bright.

Then in 2008 his behaviour changed alarmingly, and it was only a minor incident which began his decline. At 29 he was back living with his parents, and a year later he enrolled in a PTSD program.

The next five years now appear blurred, and Tim finds them difficult to recall.

"I was essentially living like a zombie,' he admitted, as the twin negative forces of grief and anger dominated his behaviour.

He now lives alone in a small house on a remote property. He struggles to get out of bed each day, and a weekly shopping trip seems like a hazardous mission.

Despite his continual feelings of despair and lethargy, Tim keeps returning to Ward 17 at Heidelberg because

"This place has shown me that I have some skillsets that I can still use...I have started looking forward again."

*

'John' is 40 years old, but feels he lost his life at 31, when he first began to relive an 'incident' which occurred when he was 18, and still 'scares him shitless'. He buried his emotions for nearly 14 years, because he felt that a 'tough guy' image defined his personality in the small town where he then lived. John now believes that if a PTSD program had been accessed soon after the incident, it could have restored his life more quickly.

John hit 'rock bottom' in 2012, when his fourth attempt at suicide failed. By then he had lost his marriage and friends, and he resided in a bush hut until his brother dragged him out of his degraded state.

"(I was) lost. I was one of the best weapons technicians in the Navy. Now it's all gone," lamented John.

He now believes that everyone needs mental support while they are in service.

"You tend to lose humanity. You lose all the things about what it is like to be human."

*

'Tony' acknowledges that PTSD situations often occur outside the military, but insists that the armed forces remain a high risk area.

"We're talking about an industry which is involved in re-making people," he explained. **"Once they get into uniform, they are reprogrammed for the best part of two years... (Unfortunately) there is no equivalent decommissioning...It is almost impossible to 'untrain'."**

*

In October 2014, ABC News Online journalist Alex Mann revealed worrying statistics about possible links between escalating crime rates and ex-servicemen suffering from various forms of PTSD. While no official figures exist about this assertion, Mann believes that between 300 - 500 war veterans are inmates in jails across the country.

Michael Quintrell is one example. He became a chronic insomniac after returning from Afghanistan in 2011, and sought comfort from the drug ice. Soon he was an addict, and the retired soldier participated in a violent robbery, which left an alleged drug dealer bleeding profusely from knife wounds.

Quintrell initially fled from the crime scene with his accomplices, but he soon returned and took his seriously injured victim to a nearby hospital. There he was arrested and ultimately sentenced to eight years in jail.

Soldiers in Afghanistan

Thirty-one year-old Lance Corporal Beau King narrowly avoided the same fate. He was discharged from the army in

2008, after serving three tours of duty in active war zones. In Afghanistan Beau King saw his friend, Michael Liddiard, lose an arm and an eye after stepping on a concealed land mine. Soon after leaving army ranks, Beau's life spiralled out of control.

"I couldn't physically take any more...that was it... My anger levels went through the roof."

Binge drinking and brawling became the defining parts of Beau King's life. After being charged three times with drink driving offences, a magistrate warned him that further offences would result in a custodial sentence being applied. Beau King is now being treated for PTSD, and hopes to overcome his behavioural demons.

Ian 'Patch' Campbell has done a 'stretch or two' behind bars, before being treated for his PTSD problem. Now Patch is the head of Adelaide's Ex-Military Rehabilitation Centre, and he regularly visits as many as 16 war veterans who are in jail, before the courts, or on parole.

Awareness of war veterans' readjustment problems is growing, and the Queensland RSL has been a trail blazer in a reform movement. This group spawned 'Mates4Mates', a welfare organisation which opened a new Family Recovery Centre for war veterans in Hobart in October 2014.

The Australian Defence Force (ADF) is now more likely to 'de-brief' personnel soon after a military operation has ended, and a recently formed suicide data base program will identify those at risk more accurately. A remedy is certainly needed: within military personnel 8.3% suffer from some form of PTSD compared to 5.2% in the wider community.

Suicide prevention programs are now more readily available to curb the rate of self-inflicted deaths in the war service community. Never-the-less, mental health problems among ex-service personnel remain a huge problem.

The stoic example of Major Garret Adcock has already been featured in chapter three of this book. In his frequent written comments from World War I's Western Front, the former Rutherglen resident was consistently critical about the competence of British officers. In all other matters pertaining to the war, he seemingly remained steadfast and loyal.

However in 1931, (12 years after the Great War ended, when Adcock had returned to his engineering career), he wrote some perceptive comments about problems all war veterans faced on their return to civilian life. Adcock's reflections, along with some other veterans' thoughts found in this book, feature strongly in Bill Gammage's excellent 1974 publication titled *The Broken Years*. Gammage, (AM), is a highly respected Australian author and historian, who received the Prime Minister's Literary Award in 2012.

Below are extracts from Adcock's insightful post-war analysis.

"**...Demobilisation meant the commencement of an era harder than war...**

A greater upheaval than from peace to war... Some were installed in 'steady jobs'...and many condemned, when they did not settle down... The comradeship of war was lost in peace. Men who lived together as brothers, sharing every danger and privation, drifted apart in peace... Those two factors, 'women' and 'possessions', which only occupy the background in war, came between friends.

The Peace following a War is worse than the War."

Nearly a century has elapsed since Major Adcock expressed

these opinions, but adjustment problems still exist today for many returning from active service.

Former commando Terry Thomas served Australia proudly in Afghanistan, but he now admits that one of the biggest battles he fought occurred after he left the armed services and returned home.

Depression and suicidal thoughts dominated his life, before he finally sought professional help.

Terry Thomas is now a Mates4Mates liaison officer and strongly believes in the benefits of regular communication for those confronted with PTSD problems.

"The most powerful thing we have on this planet is not a weapon. It's actually a conversation," Thomas recently asserted.

*

Sergeant Maurice Vincent Buckley, (alias Gerald Sexton), was one of many war veterans who exhibited erratic behaviour, both on the battle-front and in civilian life. Buckley's military career began badly. He originally

trained in a Light Horse Battalion in Egypt, before being sent back to Victoria's Langwarrin Army Camp after contracting venereal disease in Cairo. Buckley absconded from Langwarrin, and while he was absent without Leave (AWOL) he was classified as a deserter.

Sergeant Maurice Vincent Buckley,

In 1916 Buckley re-enlisted with the AIF under the name of 'Sexton', which was his mother's maiden name.

In August of that same year, his bravery on World War I's Western Front gained 'Sexton' a Distinguished Service Medal. Then, while serving with the 13th Battalion at Le Verquier in France, Sergeant Buckley effectively used his gun to clear enemy troops. He later shot an entire machine gun crew while being attacked by heavy gun fire. Buckley also made a German trench inoperable with a mortar bomb attack. By the end of the day he had captured 100 prisoners, and his extraordinary bravery was rewarded with a VC.

Later, before King George V presented him with his VC medal at Buckingham Palace, Sergeant Maurice Buckley revealed his true identity.

Previously, when World War 1 began, the AIF received more volunteers than was required. However by 1916, the response to war service duties had significantly declined, and the AIF lacked the number of service personnel it needed.

Labor Prime Minister Billy Hughes was one of several noteworthy people who advocated compulsory military conscription to solve the man-power problem. In particular he targeted Australian men between the ages of 18 and 44, and rashly promised Britain 50,000 more Australian troops. A personal 'Call to Arms' letter was distributed to all households to help stimulate support for his proposal.

However such propaganda attempts failed, because on 28th October 1916, the nation's eligible voters narrowly vetoed conscription for military service after it was put to a referendum vote.

Prime Minister Hughes responded by leaving the Labor Party, starting the Nationalist Party, and re-submitting the conscription issue to voters in 1917. On this occasion the proposal was more strongly rejected.

The then Catholic Archbishop of Melbourne was Daniel Mannix, an influential public figure, who strongly supported the anti-conscription movement. In 1920 he helped organise a St Patrick's Day protest march, and Maurice Buckley, along with other Irish-Australian VC winners, marched in the large Melbourne parade.

A year later the unpredictable Buckley recklessly accepted a bet to jump his horse over a railway gate. The risky leap was unsuccessful, and Buckley sustained serious injuries which needlessly ended his life after a 12 day stay in hospital.

The adventurous 31-year-old's coffin was accompanied by ten other VC recipients as pall bearers. After his funeral service, Maurice Vincent Buckley was laid to rest in Melbourne's Brighton Cemetery.

*

"(He had) that strange dazed stare of war…"
(Channel Two series *The War that Changed Us* - 19th August, 2014)

James Frederick Rule was so mentally scarred by his ghastly World War I experiences, that he was unable to attend his local Anzac Day marches for many years. Rule fought with the 11th Battalion of the 3rd Brigade, which made the first Anzac landing at Gallipoli on 25th April 1915. Rule seldom spoke about his war service memories, but he once divulged that 'several of his mates died in his arms', in the slaughter which accompanied the Anzac's arrival.

He was later treated several times in a military hospital for Barcoo Rot, which was a painful type of ulcer. Rule's only pleasurable war memory, was sharing a bar of dark chocolate with a few English soldiers.

In April 1916 James Rule was transferred to the Anzac Provost Corps, which performed military police duties. He was moved to England, where he married a local nurse named Lily. The couple soon moved to Western Australia. There, before the war commenced, James Rule had been studying theology, but he worked in various other occupations around Perth after being repatriated. Lily died from TB in 1933, and James Rule later married Isabella.

The mentally scarred Rule was remembered as being a committed environmentalist, before he died from a massive heart attack at the age of 78.

*

War time action certainly produced adrenalin surges in Tom Brown's behaviour. He served with the 20th Battalion in World War I, and on 6th July 1918 at Villers Bretonneau in France, Corporal Walter Thomas Brown's advance party came under sniper fire after seizing an enemy trench. Despite being subjected to heavy fire, Brown charged towards the Germans with two small bombs. He felled an enemy soldier with his fist, while 12 other Germans heeded Brown's bomb threat and surrendered.

Tom Brown was awarded a VC for his display of reckless bravery. Brown married and fathered two children after returning to civilian life in Australia.

However during World War II, the adventurous then 54-year-old from Leeton surprisingly re-enlisted for armed service, after convincing authorities he was only 39.

In the Pacific war Brown was probably KIA in Singapore, though there are two versions about the belligerent Australian's death.

Many maintain that he was shot dead after walking towards armed Japanese soldiers with grenades in his hand, shouting 'No surrender for me!' Others believe that he lost his life after organising an escape from Japanese captors.

It is known that Brown's body was never recovered, and today a memorial plaque in Leeton honours the wartime courage of this unpredictable hero.

*

The Korean War began nearly five years after World War II ended. Three hundred Australians were killed and 1,200 wounded in that protracted and frustrating campaign. Despite suffering such a huge casualty rate, the Korean War has since been called 'the forgotten war', as little changed once hostilities ceased. Capitalist South Korea and the communist state of North Korea still remain, and the border which separates these two fierce rivals is still the 38th parallel, more than 60 years after armed conflict first began.

Australia became actively involved soon after North Korean forces invaded the southern area of the Korean Peninsula, with Prime Minister Menzies pledging navy vessels and ground troops to assist our American allies.

Helping South Korean forces defend the Kapyong Valley became one of the first assignments for Australian and Canadian soldiers, and the task was indeed formidable. Approximately 1,400 of these British Commonwealth soldiers were asked to defend important strategic positions, against at least 10,000 enemy troops. The battle for Kapyong peaked on the night of 23rd April 1950. Ben O'Dowd, the Acting Commander of the RAR Regiment, vividly recalled the enemy's frightening 'build ups' to various battles.

"When the (sound of) bugles and whistles stopped, we knew they were on their way... Some of their soldiers did not carry (conventional) weapons - just buckets of grenades."

By next morning, the four Australian companies were forced to withdraw, leaving much carnage behind them. Thirty-two diggers were KIA, and a further 53 wounded, but the enemy lost a massive 500 soldiers.

The Americans honoured the Australian RAR Battalion with a Silver Star for its outstanding performance. However the crucial contribution of Commander O'Dowd, who one war correspondent claimed had achieved 'a superb military feat', was never mentioned in despatches, though many Australian lives were saved in his well- planned withdrawal.

If the Korean conflict was 'the forgotten war', the decade long struggle for control of Vietnam, became 'the controversial war'. Between the 1960s and early 1970s, the Vietnam War became a topic which was fiercely debated within Australian society. The issue finally split the nation, and caused social disruption which had not been witnessed since the conscription debate of World War I. Many draft resistors, conscientious objectors and protestors were either fined or jailed, and some Vietnam War veterans unfortunately received hostile receptions after they arrived home.

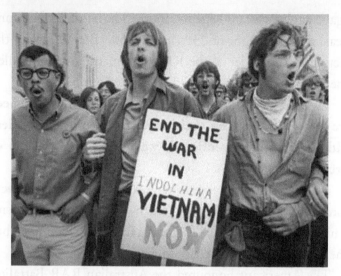

Vietnam War demonstrations

Many believe that Australia's involvement in this war was politically based, claiming that we were only there to honour the American alliance.

The commitment of many countries was also influenced by the 'domino theory'. This term described the belief, that if communism became established in one country, then neighbouring nations would more easily follow their example. This would further endanger the 'capitalist' life style favoured by Western world countries like Australia.

In 1962 authorities sent armed advisers to trouble spots in Vietnam, and in November 1963, after the American backed President Diem and his brother were both assassinated, our armed support increased.

In 1964 the Australian government introduced conscription for military service. It was an unprecedented decision, as previous World War I government attempts to gain this change had twice been rejected in referendums by Australian voters.

Under the new National Service scheme, all Australian 20-year-old men were required to register with the Department of Labour and National Service (DLNS). The applicants then became subject to a bi-annual ballot, which many likened to a 'chook raffle'.

Private Errol Noack

If the applicant's birth date matched a numbered marble, which was drawn at random from a barrel, the 'successful' applicant was selected for compulsory military service. This commitment required two years of continuous service in the army, followed by three years of part-time service with the Army Reserve. A later amendment to the Parliamentary Act added the proviso that any serviceman involved in full-time service became eligible for overseas missions.

Initially over half the population supported these arbitrary government policies. Then, in June 1966, Private Errol Noack became the first conscripted soldier to be KIA in Vietnam. This fatality possibly became the catalyst for change. Public anti-war sentiments became more strident, as the returning number of 'body bags' continued to grow.

"And can you tell me doctor, why I still can't get to sleep?
And night-time's just a jungle dark and a barking M 16?
And what's this rash that comes and goes
Can you tell me what it means?
God help me, I was only nineteen."

(Extracts from John Schumann's song, *I Was Only Nineteen*)

*

In 1968 a then 19-year-old Michael 'Mick' Bergin was accidentally caught up in the controversy surrounding Vietnam, when he was conscripted for national service. The teenager from the Melbourne suburb of Ormond was then an apprentice carpenter, and only six months short of completing his trade qualifications. Fortunately Mick was able to complete his apprenticeship, after being granted permission to defer his military service.

His three-month basic army service was completed at Puckapunyal Army Camp, and Mick then began a course at Liverpool near Sydney with the School of Military Engineering (SME). There he learned road building and river crossing techniques, and Mick also gained experience with various explosive devices. Jungle training was then undertaken at Kanundra in Queensland, before Mick returned to SME in a holding situation, prior to receiving an overseas posting.

On 30th June 1970 the young conscripted soldier was flown to Saigon, the capital of South Vietnam. Sapper Michael Bergin was then transferred to the headquarters of 1 Field Squadron in Nui Dat, where he was based for his 12 month tour of duty.

Ongoing nervous tension and unpredictable outcomes

Sapper Mick Bergin

characterised most days during that eventful year. At times Mick and his army mates would accompany Army Personnel Carriers, (APCs), through potentially dangerous village areas. They also walked with infantry troops, and escorted tanks on battle missions. They never knew when they would have an explosives problem to overcome, or whether they would be ambushed by hidden enemy forces. Therefore, life was constantly 'lived on the edge', and the Diggers were always alert to life threatening scenarios which could suddenly erupt around them.

In this nerve-racking environment, Mick was sustained by his religious beliefs, and he regularly confided with army chaplains when they visited Nui Dat. The strong spirit of mateship, which developed in 1 Field Squadron, was also a vital element for Mick's emotional welfare.

Mick was affected by Post-Traumatic Stress Disorder, (PTSD), after he returned to Australia in July 1971, and many work related issues became irritating and trivial for the front-line war veteran.

After Mick and Marie's seven children reached adulthood, the couple purchased a rural property in East Gippsland. Mick now cherishes the tranquility and independence of farm life, and his children and grandchildren often share enjoyable holidays with them at 'the block'. Mick also values the regular consultations he has with a Department of Veteran Affairs (DVA) psychiatrist.

The comradeship of his army mates remains essential for Mick's emotional stability. Reunions and events organised by the Victorian Tunnel Rats Association, help to reinforce his belief that war veterans are always there for their mates in time of need.

Mick Bergin with grandson Isaac

Mick still fondly recalls the 'welcome home' reunion, which coincided with the 25th anniversary of the Vietnam tour of duty. On that memorable day, a seemingly endless line of Vietnam War veterans stretched well beyond the boundaries of Sydney's Hyde Park.

On the centenary of Anzac Day, 25th April 2015, Mick and his army mates re-assembled in Darwin.

*

The late 'Michael Ryan', (name changed at the request of family members) was also affected by PTSD, after he returned from the Vietnam conflict. This third son of four brothers, from the Melbourne's northern suburbs, had previously been a Royal Australian Navy, (RAN) Diver, but was working in a timber yard when he received his 'call up' to military service in 1967.

Michael was a fun-loving lad, who had previously played football with the Collingwood under 19s team, and this likeable extrovert embraced army life with much enthusiasm. He was assigned to the 5th Battalion of the Royal Australian Engineers, (RAR), and between 1969 and 1970 Private Michael Ryan undertook a tour of duty in Vietnam.

The 5th RAR Battalion was a successful unit. They participated in 16 major operations, and defeated a heavily armed Viet Cong group which was defending Binh Ba. They also participated in 31 battalion sized operations, which included nine cordons and searches of villages in the Phouk Tuy province. At times the villages were deserted, but the RAR knew the enemy lurked somewhere close by beneath the ground in their elaborate tunnel system. Brave Aussie 'tunnel rats' begun to discover these fortified hidden communities.

In that ever-dangerous environment Michael twice came perilously close to becoming another Vietnam casualty. He deliberately drew fire from an armed group of the enemy, so one of his wounded army mates could be dragged to safety. The other incident occurred during Operation Camden, when a grenade exploded behind him. Michael suffered serious shrapnel wounds to his back. During his later recovery period in Australia, it was decided that Private Michael Ryan would not return to the south-east Asian conflict.

In civilian life, it became increasingly apparent that Michael was suffering from PTSD. He found it almost impossible to stand in queues, or visit crowded shopping centres. Entering underground car parks reminded him of the Viet Cong's underground tunnel communities.

Michael was constantly anxious in his demeanour, and insisted on facing any nearby door when dining in a restaurant. He also shared the belief with other Viet veterans, that many of the general public, and some Second World War veterans at RSL clubs, devalued the worth of what Australian service personnel had achieved in Vietnam. A Melbourne traffic accident, which led to a partial amputation of one leg, also affected his physical and mental health.

Problems also arose in various work locations. Michael deliberately avoided promotional opportunities, and reminders of the traumatic past flooded back when Vietnamese work colleagues cooked their traditional food during lunch breaks. Alcohol temporarily became an escape mechanism for his haunting memories, but in 1995 Michael Ryan suffered some form of a mental break down. He was ruled medically unfit to continue in the work force, and became a voluntary patient at the Heidelberg Repatriation Hospital.

Michael seemingly recovered well from this setback, and he remained close to his loyal wife, five children, and many Vietnam veterans. Reunions were important in the gradual healing process, but such occasions were often preceded by a long and stressful build-up of emotions. He seldom spoke about his war experiences, and never encouraged his children to pursue military careers.

His general health continued to decline, and in May 2010 the 62-year-old Michael Ryan suffered a life ending heart attack.

*

Warrant Officer Ted Baulch (far left) with two armymates

Edward Frederick ('Ted') Baulch was raised on a dairy farm near Victoria's Otway Ranges. A strong military background exists among the Baulchs, as ten of his extended family served in Tobruk and on the Kokoda Trail during World War II. Fortunately all the 'Baulch boys' returned from their overseas military service, and Ted's favourite uncle would often share his war experiences with his nephew.

During his early employment years, Ted drove his father's tip truck, but in 1954, after serving three months of compulsory national service, Ted Baulch enlisted in the Australian Army.

He was initially stationed at Kapooka Army Camp in NSW, but then transferred to Puckapunyal where he completed a driver's training course. During the next 12 years of army service Ted Baulch was assigned to Melbourne's Victoria Barracks, and he was also based for a time in Papua-New Guinea.

From 22nd April 1966 until 19th April 1967, he was assigned to the 87th Transport Platoon of the Royal Australian Army Corps in Vietnam. Over 500 young Australian lives were lost in the Vietnam conflict, and serving in that war-torn South-East Asian country was an unnerving experience. The smiling local villagers by day could become Viet Cong killers at night, so Ted and his army mates were ever watchful. Armed escorts accompanied them on their regular road building or driving exercises, and signs of danger in the steamy jungle environment were often present.

Ted endured especially harrowing experiences, when he temporarily replaced a Non-Commissioned Officer, (NCO), in Saigon. There he saw Buddhist protestors setting themselves on fire, and he also witnessed public executions. Today, nearly 50 years later, flashbacks and broken sleep from these confronting experiences still haunt Ted Baulch.

Ted ended his Vietnam tour of duty in April 1967. Some of his Digger mates have returned for holiday visits, while a few married local women and settled in Vietnam. Ted, Mick

Bergin, and the late Michael Ryan, never considered making a return visit.

After finishing his overseas stint, Ted served in the Army for a further eight years. As a Platoon Sergeant, he was responsible for the development of 15 young soldiers at Puckapunyal, and he also undertook short-term relief duties at other army locations.

Warrant Officer Ted Baulch (centre of the group)

In 1975, Warrant Officer Class1 Edward Frederick Baulch retired from the Australian army after serving his country proudly for 30 years. During that time he became the recipient of seven medals, with the Vietnam Service Medal being the most prestigious.

Recently, when Ted travelled back to his old stamping ground of Apollo Bay, he discovered that his elderly aunt had precariously placed her late husband's military medals on a wall in her house. Ted persuaded her to allow him to have the medals mounted professionally, and his grateful relative wore these now secure and very presentable medals, at the very next Apollo Bay Anzac Day march.

"He returned a changed man. He had a shorter fuse, and a longer gaze."

(Maria Rowe, wife of Vietnam veteran, Bill Rowe)

Bill Rowe joined the Air Force in 1956, and he volunteered for a tour of duty in Vietnam in April 1970. Two factors motivated his decision. He 'stood in' for a mate whose wife was opposed to her husband's involvement, and he was attracted by the perks which would then become available, such as generous home loan opportunities.

However everything went 'pear shaped' during that 11 month mission in Vietnam. Physically, Bill sustained shrapnel wounds to his face and arms. Mentally he was traumatised by the memory of a close mate, who died after accidentally firing a shot through his jaw and into his skull.

Bill Rowe returned, but he was very different. The 'new' Bill often suffered from panic attacks and moods of angry frustration.

"At the age of 31, I was a changed man," he admitted.

Bill remained in denial about his health for a decade. During that time he shunned the activities and help of the Vietnam veteran's community until 1995, which was the year of his retirement. He then sought assistance, and in 1997 he was diagnosed with a form of PTSD.

A new challenge possibly looms, as the now 75-year-old Bill Rowe is participating in a study which is investigating possible links between PTSD and Alzheimer's disease.

"One of the common symptoms of Alzheimer's disease is memory disturbance. ...and this occurs in the same region of the brain that has disturbances from a PTSD... There might be a link," stated Professor Malcolm Hopwood, one of the investigating experts.

A three year study is being conducted on this possible connection.

6

WORLD WAR 1 CASE STUDY 2 -
ALBERT BORELLA (VC),
A CALM HERO

Lieutenant Albert Chalmers Borella became Australia's oldest VC recipient during World War I. This calm, determined and righteous man was 37 years of age when he received the prestigious honour, which stemmed from his exceptional acts of bravery on the Western Front. Borella is also credited with currently being the Northern Territory's only VC winner.

Bert Borella was a conservative man, but his life experiences were both diverse and adventurous. In his early years he faced the possibility of economic ruin, before he resolutely travelled over a hundred kilometres through the Australian outback to enlist for war service. He sat for Parliament, he produced four children after marrying at the age of 47, and he was 58 years of age when he volunteered for World War II service.

Albert Borella was born into a farming family near Bendigo. He also became a local farmer, and for an 18 month period Bert was a part-time soldier with the Victorian Rangers. In 1910 Bert Borella came to Melbourne, where he worked for three years as a fire fighter with the Melbourne Metropolitan Fire Brigade.

After seeing a newspaper advertisement regarding a land

ballot at Daly River in the Northern Territory, he and two friends soon purchased a farming allotment. Bert farmed the land at Daly River for two years, but when government assistance stalled, his territorial farming future appeared bleak. Consequently, Bert gained employment at Tennant Creek as a cook with a survey team, shortly before the outbreak of World War I.

In January 1915 Bert Borella began an epic journey in his quest to sign up for military service. Borella, (and possibly an Aboriginal local called Charlie), doggedly walked and swam through flooded rivers in the humid outback heat to Powell Creek near Renner Springs. There he borrowed a horse, and rode 500 kilometres further to Katherine. Bert then travelled north to Pine Creek on a mail coach, before finally catching a train to Darwin.

At 'the top end' Bert Borella's determination was tested further, as there were no national recruitment centres in the Northern Territory. The resilient man refused to give up his enlistment dream. He sailed from Darwin to Townsville, and it was in that Queensland city, on 8th March 1915, that

Albert Borella finally succeeded in volunteering for service with the Australian Army.

After arriving in Gallipoli with the 26th Battalion, Private Borella only served two months in the Dardanelles before being evacuated after contracting jaundice. Recognition and promotion came quickly for him after he resumed

Albert Borella VC   armed action in Europe's Western

Front on 5th February 1916. On 11th May 1917 Borella received a Military Cross, and by August of that year he was promoted to the rank of Lieutenant. This resulted in him completing an officer's training course in England. After returning to the Western Front, Lieutenant Borella's most famous war achievement occurred in July 1918 at Villers Bretonneau in France.

On July 17th Borella's platoon was heavily outnumbered, but the steely officer shot two enemy machine gun operators with his revolver. Borella then ran ahead of his group and, despite being under heavy enemy fire, captured a German machine gun and cleared a trench and dugout. Aided by two Lewis guns, Borella's group, which was then reduced to ten in number, launched a series of aggressive trench engagements. In these inspired counter-attacks, Albert Borella proved to be deadly accurate with his revolver and rifle, and 30 enemy soldiers were captured by his platoon.

Lieutenant Albert Borella was awarded a VC, which was personally presented to him by King George V at Sandringham in England, on 16th September 1918. Albert Borella's three brothers also volunteered for World War I service, and they all fortunately returned safely to Australia.

Bert Borella returned to farming on a soldier settlement block near Hamilton in Western Victoria. At the age of 47 he married Elsie Jane Love, and in 1924 he became the National Party candidate for the state seat of Dundas.

Borella's attempted move into politics was not successful, but at the age of 58 he was accepted for World War II home duties with the Australian Army. He rose to the rank of captain in this conflict. After being demobilised, Borella became a public servant, before relocating to the NSW border town of Albury, where he remained until his death in 1968. Borella Road in North Albury is named in his honour. In the year he died, a plaque detailing Borella's wartime deeds was unveiled at Jingli in the Northern Territory.

Albert Borella lived until he was 86, and throughout his long life his four children never heard their father mention his war experiences. Rowan Borella recalls that his dad was a quiet and reserved man, who had a special affection for Anzac Day celebrations. For years Bert Borella would be picked up by friends at 5 a.m. for the Anzac dawn service on Monument Hill in Albury, and he would not return home until late that night.

Mary and Rowan Borella

Rowan Borella is now aged in his early 80s. He remains unsure about what motivated his father to produce his incredible acts of bravery in combat situations, but suspects that it was his sense of duty as platoon leader, which steeled him to set a brave example for the men he commanded.

Between 20th February and 3rd March 2015, the centenary of Albert Borella's famous journey through the Australian outback was re-enacted. The Federal Government, as part of its 100th year of Anzac Day celebrations, contributed 1.7

million dollars to the Northern Territory government, to help cover costs for a prestigious event named the Borella Ride.

Four riders undertook the same journey which Albert Borella took 100 years ago. The war hero's grandson, Richard Borella, was one of the participants, while Rowan Borella and his wife Mary accompanied the main group in a campervan vehicle.

The first stage of the re-enacted pilgrimage was a 160 kilometre walk. Then a 504 kilometre horse journey took the four riders to Katherine, and the epic 11 day mission culminated with a train ride from Pine Creek to Darwin.

Tennant Creek, Renner Springs, Elliott, Newcastle Waters, Dunmarra, Daly Waters, Larrimah and Mataranka were other settlements which the riders visited. An educational team, (headed by historian Tom Lewis), accompanied the riders and provided interesting details for tourists, school children and residents of settlements.

At Elliott on February 23rd, the participants enjoyed a community based sausage sizzle, and welcome functions were also held at other settlements on the journey.

Adam Giles, the Chief Minister of the Northern Territory, met the travellers at East Arm Station, and announced that a new suburb in Palmerston near Darwin would be named after the famous VC winner.

Finally, on March 3rd, at Darwin's Stokes Hill Wharf, members of the general public dressed in 1915 theme costume,

Richard Borella

walked the last three kilometres of the epic journey with the weary but satisfied travellers. Keith Payne, a VC veteran from the Vietnam War, and television legend Ray Martin, were there to greet all the participants at the journey's end.

The overall experience provided Richard Borella with fresh insights about the famous grandfather he had only known as a small child.

"It really gave me a picture of how mentally strong he must have been," was his comment before he enjoyed a well-earned cold beer.

7

OTHER STOIC AUSTRALIAN LEGENDS

"...The whole AIF came to look upon him as a rock of strength that never failed. We of the 14th Battalion never ceased to be thrilled when we...heard ourselves referred to as 'some of Jacka's mob'."

(Sentiments expressed by an anonymous member of the 14th Battalion).

Captain Albert (Bert) Jacka was Gallipoli's first and most famous VC winner. His fearless bravery elevated him to legendary status among his 14th Battalion comrades, the general public and future VC recipients.

Bert Jacka was one of seven children sired by a Victorian share farmer and haulage contractor. The relationship between Bert and his father, Nathaniel Jacka, was often volatile, as the moody parent was an ardent socialist. He deplored both Australia's involvement in 'an imperialist war', and moves towards conscripting young men for military service. His much acclaimed son, however, believed that conscription was essential to gain victory in World War I. When the highly decorated Albert Jacka returned from overseas duties to a hero's public welcome in Melbourne, Nathaniel Jacka was not present at the celebrations.

In combat situations Bert Jacka was a fearless fighting machine, and his brave instincts became obvious shortly after the Anzacs first landed at Galllipoli. On 19th May 1915 Bert Jacka, and three other members of the 14th Battalion, unsuccessfully attempted a frontal attack on a Turkish trench. Jacka reacted to the setback by crawling through 'no man's land' behind the enemy, and launching a surprise assault. The formidable Australian killed five of the foe with his revolver, and accounted for another two with his knife.

Shortly after enemy gunfire stopped, Lieutenant Crabbe, the commanding officer in charge, discovered Jacka with a cigarette dangling from his mouth, and seven enemy corpses sprawled near him in the trench.

"Well, I managed to get the beggars sir" was Bert's alleged comment.

Jacka's heroic reputation continued to grow. At Pozieres, near the Somme on Europe's Western Front, his presence of mind and unflinching courage virtually saved the day for allied forces, after their line of resistance was broken by German forces. Despite being knocked to the ground, and suffering wounds to the head and shoulders, Jacka killed approximately 20 enemy soldiers. His daring intervention rescued his captive mates, and was later described as being

"... the most dramatic act of individual audacity in the history of the A.I.F."

Albert Jacka VC

Two military medals (MMs) were added to Jacka's impressive military awards in Western Front battles, but noted war correspondent, C.E.W. Bean, believes that Albert Jacka should have received two bars to his existing VC award. Despite his imposing record, Albert Jacka was never promoted beyond the rank of captain. Perhaps his abrasive manner was too blunt for the military establishment.

Jacka was gifted five hundred pounds and a gold medal by controversial Melbourne businessman John Wren, after serious war wounds forced the shy hero to return to Australia. In civilian life Albert Jacka operated a Melbourne electrical goods and exporting business, and in 1921 he married his work secretary, Frances Veronica ('Vera') Carey. The couple raised an adopted daughter named Elizabeth ('Betty'), and Bert Jacka became a popular Mayor of St. Kilda. In this role he gained much respect for welfare measures he established for less fortunate people in the community.

Albert Jacka appeared to cope well mentally and emotionally with his combat experiences, but several severe war wounds rapidly eroded his physical health, and the esteemed warrior died prematurely at the age of 39.

Eight fellow Australian VC winners were pall bearers at Albert Jacka's funeral, while past members of his brigade and many poor and unemployed people walked behind the hearse on that stiflingly hot January day in 1932. Overall at least 6,000 admirers witnessed his journey to St. Kilda cemetery, and today visitors can read the following epitaph which honours this pragmatic hero.

"Captain Albert Jacka
VC, MC and Bar, 14ᵗʰ Battalion A.I.F.
The first VC in the Great War 1914-1918.
A gallant soldier,
An honoured citizen."

Overall, when the events of Bert Jacka's life are evaluated,

Lance Corporal
Leonard Keysor VC

this modest man coped successfully with his war experiences, and was able to lead a relatively normal existence after returning to civilian life. The same conclusion applies to many other combat heroes from various wars.

Lance-Corporal Leonard Keysor from the 1st Battalion was another VC recipient at Gallipoli, who conspicuously defended his army mates. For almost 50 hours Keysor risked his own life, while throwing back Turkish bombs which endangered his unit's forward trenches. The English born Keysor was wounded twice during exchanges, but he survived various battles at Gallipoli and later on the Western Front.

Following his war experiences, Leonard Keysor became a fierce opponent of conscription. He returned to London after the war, where he married and became a successful businessman. The 65-year old stoic warrior left a widow and daughter, after he lost his battle with cancer.

*

Lieutenant Arthur
Blackburn

Lieutenant Arthur Seaford Blackburn enlisted in the 10th Battalion at the age of 21, after graduating in Law from Adelaide University in 1913. His group was among the first to land at Gallipoli, and during the arduous campaign, Blackburn was promoted to the rank of Second Lieutenant.

His first battalion Battalion later became involved in heavy Western Front action at Pozieres in France on 23rd July 1918. In the fierce battle, Blackburn led four successive bombing raids, which gained over 300 metres of enemy territory.

Arthur Blackburn received a VC for the valour he displayed at Pozieres, but shortly afterwards injuries forced him to return to Australia. He then married, resumed his legal career, and staunchly supported the pro-conscription campaign. Between 1921 and 1923 Arthur Blackburn was the National Party Member for Sturt in the South Australian Parliament.

He returned to active service with the advent of World War II, but unfortunately spent three years in a Japanese POW camp. Arthur Blackburn (VC, CMG, CBE, ED) was 68 when he passed away in Adelaide.

*

Corporal William ('Bill') Dunstan unknowingly teamed up with two other Australian VC recipients, when he joined the 7th Battalion at Gallipoli. Lieutenant Frederick Tubb, Corporal Alexander Burton and Dunstan, all gained this revered honour, after continually defending a barricade they had erected. Enemy bombs frequently demolished their sandbag defence base, which was reconstructed many times during the fierce attacks.

Corporal William Dunstan VC

Diggers serving in Afghanistan during the early years of the 21st century probably used mobile phones or iPads to record events. Digital cameras may have been used to store photographic memoirs for those serving in Vietnam, but on World War I battlefields, accounts of events were noted in personal letters and diaries. Legendary World War I leader Harry 'Pompei' Elliott told his wife that

"Your letters are an inspiration," and in general the morale of troops improved when letters arrived from home.

Fred Tubb, an extroverted and diminutive grazier from Longwood in north-east Victoria, regularly wrote diary entries about the carnage surrounding him at Gallipoli. Below are extracts Tubb recorded after he became one of three Australians who were awarded VC's in the same battle. This honour originated from a brutal confrontation at Lone Pine on 10th August 1915.

"I was extremely lucky, and feel grateful for being alive and able to write... It is miraculous that I am still alive. Three different times I was blown yards away from bombs. Burton of Euroa deserves the highest praise for his gallant action, for three times filling a breach...till they killed him...a lot more of our good old 7th are gone."

Burton received a posthumous VC, after being killed by a sniper's bullet, Tubb later died at the age of 35 from serious injuries he sustained at Gallipoli and on the Western Front, and Dunstan was temporarily blinded in the fierce attacks at Lone Pine.

Bill Dunstan's partial blindness lasted for almost a year, but the former messenger boy for a Ballarat

Frederick Tubb

grocer overcame his war injuries, and soon became highly successful in civilian life.

Dunstan had risen to the rank of Lieutenant when he left the army service in 1928. He went on to become the General Manager of the *Herald* and *Weekly Times* newspaper group. Bill Dunstan was highly respected in business, judicial and parliamentary circles, but this reserved man shunned any public recognition of his wartime achievements. A memorial erected in his honour still stands in Sturt Street Ballarat, and the 'Dunstan VC Club' at Puckapunyal operates to this day.

On 23rd August 1918 Lieutenant William Donovan Joynt rendered outstanding service, while serving as an officer with the 8th Battalion at Herleville Wood near Chuignes in France.

Joynt reorganised a 6th Battalion unit which had lost its officers in battle. He continually urged them to advance, and the group captured a German post and 50 prisoners. Battalion members then moved to within 50 metres of an enemy machine gun post, and captured the leader and other German soldiers at pistol point. Joynt himself sustained wounds in the three day battle which followed.

For 60 years William Joynt (VC), worked as a printer and publisher after returning to civilian life. He married at the age of 43, and became active in local government matters around Berwick on the south-eastern fringe of Melbourne. William Joynt also wrote three books, titled *Saving the Channel Ports, Breaking the Road for Rest* and *To Russia and back through Communist Countries.*

Lieutenant William Donovan Joynt

He was 97 when he died in the Melbourne suburb of Windsor.

*

Lance-Corporal
Walter Peeler

Lance-Corporal Walter ('Wally') Peeler was a member of the 3rd Pioneer Battalion, which was involved in a fierce encounter at Broodseinde near Ypres in Belgium on 4th October 1917.

Wally Peeler was instrumental in pushing back German soldiers into a shell hole, and he personally accounted for nine of the enemy forces. Peeler continued his successful assaults, and his unit was able to advance and gain more enemy casualties. It is estimated that Lance-Corporal Peeler 'neutralised' 30 German soldiers in these dangerous battles.

The mild-mannered and friendly Wally Peeler (VC) became a custodian at Melbourne's Shrine of Remembrance when he returned to civilian life. He died at the age of 81.

*

Sergeant William ('Rusty') Ruthven was a member of the 23rd Battalion which became involved in a battle at Ville-Sur-Ancre in France on 19th May 1918.

When his Battalion advanced significant losses were suffered, and Sergeant Ruthven's commanding officer was seriously wounded, so Rusty Ruthven assumed command.

His impact was immediate. Sergeant Ruthven bombed an enemy post, and seized a gun from a German he had bayoneted. With that weapon he wounded two other Germans, and captured six others. In later action the inspirational VC recipient killed two other enemy soldiers, and forced another 32 to surrender. For the reminder of the day, as bullets whizzed around him, the gallant Collingwood

Sergeant William Ruthven

hero continually encouraged his men to consolidate their position.

In civilian life, Ruthven was a mechanical engineer, and he later served as a Labor politician for 16 years. He was 77 when he died in 1970.

*

Lieutenant Percy Valentine Storkey was born in New Zealand, and was a University student when he enlisted in the AIF in 1915.

On the Western Front Storkey served as an officer with the 19th Battalion, which came under fierce fire at Hangard Wood in France on 7th April 1914.

Storkey's group of 13 men was confronted by approximately 80 German soldiers, but they killed three officers and killed or wounded another 30-50 enemy soldiers.

When the war ended Percy Storkey completed his law studies, and joined a legal practice. He later became a judge, and died in England at the age of 78.

*

Private William ('Bill') Matthew Curry was a member of the 53rd Battalion, and on 1st September 1918 at Mont St Quentin in France, the group came under heavy artillery fire from the enemy. Private Curry confronted the dangerous situation by rushing forward, killing an entire German gun crew, and capturing a machine gun. He repeated that action on the afternoon of the same day, and again inflicted heavy casualties on enemy forces. Early next morning, despite suffering from the effects of gas inhalation, Private Curry successfully guided an allied company to safety.

Bill Curry was awarded a VC for his courageous actions. In civilian life he worked as a labourer and railway worker, before becoming the NSW state Labor member of the seat of Kogarah for seven years.

Bill Curry was 57 when he passed away in Sydney.

8

WAR ERUPTS IN THE PACIFIC

On 7ᵗʰ December 1941, the simmering tensions which had existed between America and Japan since the 1930s, suddenly exploded into armed aggression. Early that morning, Japan unexpectedly launched aircraft bombing attacks on important American military targets at Pearl Harbour in Hawaii.

The carnage was horrific. Two thousand three hundred American servicemen and civilians were killed, nearly 1,200 were wounded, ten crucially important navy vessels were destroyed, and 188 aircraft wrecked during the devastating blitz.

America and Britain immediately declared war on Japan.

A fearful Australian government then lobbied 'the mother country' to have our British Empire troops returned home from the battlefields of Europe and North Africa, so the nation could prepare for the threat of a Japanese invasion.

British Prime Minister Winston Churchill strongly opposed the request. He wanted our troops deployed to Burma, where they could better defend India. He also argued that any countries in the Pacific, which temporarily fell to Japan, would quickly be regained once Germany was defeated.

Furthermore, the naval base capabilities of Singapore, ('the Gibraltar of the East'), were supposedly impregnable, and on Christmas Day 1941 Churchill boldly asserted that

"Singapore will not fall."

John Curtin, Australia's war time Prime Minister, was unconvinced, and he was also skeptical about Britain's commitment to defending our overall defence needs. His request for a stronger British defence of Singapore was ignored, so on Boxing Day 1941 Curtin made an historic public announcement about Australia's future.

"Without any inhibitions…I make it quite clear that Australia looks to America, free from any pangs as to our

traditional links… with the United Kingdom…"

In his policy changing address, Prime Minister Curtin also reminded the United States about the mutual benefits which would flow from a proposed new alliance.

"Australia is the last bastion

Winston Churchill

between the west coast of America

and the Japanese. If Australia goes, the Americas are wide open."

John Curtin

Churchill was reportedly furious about Australia's dramatic dependency shift, but Curtin's foreign policy change was soon vindicated. General Yamashita's 25th Army Battalion confused allied strategists, when their land forces attacked from countries near Singapore. The invaders easily overcame local resistance in Thailand and Malaya. A nervous Lieutenant-General Arthur Percival, the British officer commanding Malaya forces, ordered 30,000 British troops to retreat back to Singapore. This tactic resulted in the Japanese being outnumbered by an approximate ratio of 10:1: it was therefore unthinkable that Britain's heavily defended naval base could fall.

However by early 1942 key Singapore amenities, including reservoirs and the main pumping station, were in Japanese hands. Finally, on the 15th February 1942, (which was 30 days ahead of Yamashita's schedule), an unthinkable possibility became a stark reality: Lieutenant-General Percival surrendered Singapore to Japan.

Australia's commanding officer, Lieutenant-General Henry Gordon Bennett, had previously abandoned his leadership of the 8th Division and escaped from the island. In retrospect, the loss of Singapore was not surprising. The Japanese were more mobile and better organised than the more complacent allied troops, who were poorly led by both British and Australian commanders. The loss of Singapore was Britain's worst World War II defeat, and Churchill reportedly never forgave Percival for surrendering that crucial Pacific defence base.

The loss of Singapore brought grave consequences to Australia. A mammoth 15,000 Aussie servicemen became POWs, and public morale slumped across the shocked continent. Many citizens feared that the Japanese juggernaut would overwhelm Australia, and four days after Singapore fell, the already grim situation grew worse.

For the first time in Australia's short history, the continent was attacked by a foreign nation, when approximately 200 Japanese fighter planes launched a massive assault on Darwin. It was the most comprehensive air raid attack since Pearl Harbour, with at least 240 people being killed and 400 wounded in a savage 40 minute barrage. Twenty-seven ships and 80 aeroplanes were also badly damaged.

In early March 1942 more raids were made on northern settlements, with Broome, Townsville, Port Hedland, Wyndham and Derby being subjected to bombing attacks. By then Hong Kong, Malaya, Singapore and New Britain were already controlled by Japan, and the threat of a full scale invasion of Australia appeared likely. In late May 1942 Australians became more despondent about their future, after an enemy submarine attack in Sydney Harbour was attempted.

In these worrying times belligerent opposition Labor spokesperson, Eddie Ward, made an inflammatory accusation during the 1942 Federal election campaign. Ward claimed that the incumbent Menzies government was committed to abandoning all Australian territory north of Brisbane, if the Japanese invaded the mainland. Angry debate broke out across the country about the 'Brisbane line' claim, which a

1943 Royal Commission found to be unsubstantiated.

However this unsettling rumour further upset the apprehensive public, who now craved their far away volunteer soldiers to return home, and for America to play a decisive part in the Pacific conflict.

General Douglas MacArthur

Fortunately, an alliance with the United States was finalised, and American General Douglas MacArthur was appointed Supreme Commander of the South-West Pacific region. Optimism increased after American naval forces gained significant victories in the Battle of the Coral Sea, and Midway Islands. These ocean defeats increased the pressure on Japanese land forces to successfully invade New Guinea, (now Papua-New Guinea, PNG), and bring the vital Pacific Ocean outlet of Port Moresby under their control. The Australian general, Sir Thomas Blamey, was appointed as the Commander of Allied Land Forces, and his main objective was the protection of the Kokoda Trail, from where enemy land forces hoped to seize Port Moresby.

At that time, Australian military forces were seriously undermanned. Our regular troops were either locked up in Japanese POW camps or on duty in Europe or North Africa. Consequently, Australia's destiny was almost completely dependent on the 'chocolate soldiers'.

'Chocolate soldiers', or 'Chocos', were insulting terms used by career soldiers in the AIF. The term described inexperienced recruits from the Citizens Military Forces, (CMF), who had previously undertaken basic military training as a hobby. The battle hardened AIF veterans were initially skeptical about the capabilities of the 'Chocos', who were assigned to serve alongside them in the New Guinea conflict.

There is no doubt that 'the chocolate soldiers' were poorly prepared, hastily trained, few in number and basically ignorant about the formidable future challenges that lay ahead. However, until the AIF units arrived in New Guinea, they were the only available option.

Months later it was the Australian 'chocolate soldiers' in the 39th Battalion who halted the Japanese advancement along the Kokoda Trail for four crucial days, while they waited for AIF reinforcements to arrive. This brave achievement earned the 'Chocos' the respect they deserved from army mates who had previously scorned them.

*

Paul Keating

"The Australians who served in Papua New Guinea, fought and died, not for the defence of the old world, but for the new world. Their world.

They died in defence of Australia, and the civilisation which had grown up there. That is why it might be said that, for Australians, the battles in Papua New Guinea were the most important ever fought."

(Former Prime Minister Paul Keating, Bomana Cemetery, Port Moresby, Anzac Day, 1992)

9

GEORGE COPS- A PROUD SURVIVOR OF THE 39TH BATTALION

George Albert Cops was born in the small south-west Victorian town of Beeac on 28th July, 1922. He was the eldest of three children, and his English born father was a World War I veteran who served with the 59th Battalion AIF on Europe's Western Front. He suffered ill-health for years, after being wounded and gassed in the Great War, and was only 54 when he died.

The father's example motivated George Cops to become a soldier, and in July 1939 the 17-year-old grocery store employee volunteered for army service with the 23/21st Militia Battalion. A short time later, Machine Gun Company Sergeant Cops joined the newly created 39th Australian Infantry Battalion, which was soon designated to take up garrison duties in New Guinea.

On Boxing Day 1941 the 39th Battalion boarded the 'Aquitania', which berthed at Port Moresby on 3rd January 1942. George and his optimistic young army mates had been led to believe their new home would be an island paradise, with swaying

George Cops

palm trees and exotic hula dancers there to greet them.

Reality was entirely different, as they were confronted with a barren, hot, dusty and mosquito infested environment. Morale plummeted further within the Battalion, when they discovered that there was virtually no transport for the mobilisation of troops, no tents, no cooking supplies and no maps of the area.

Seven days after arriving George Cops experienced his first attack of dysentery, and spent a week in a makeshift hospital lying on a groundsheet while he recovered. This medical condition was very virulent for the soldiers during the first two months in New Guinea, as hygiene standards were poor.

Tragedy struck in June 1942 when the Burn Phillip transport ship 'Macdhui' was bombed by the Japanese in Port Moresby harbour. Shortly afterwards both Commander Lieutenant Edward Money and Sergeant Ronald Stewart died from horrendous burns they suffered during the air-raid attack.

George saw Ron Stewart on the day he passed away. His entire skin was hanging in shreds from his body, as he sought relief in a saline bath from the intense pain, and George was deeply affected by the experience. The two victims were among the first to be buried at Bomana Cemetery, which, by the war's end, became the final resting

George Cops in New Guinea

place for approximately 3,000 servicemen and women.

George vividly recalls the group's reactions to the many air raids they experienced in Port Moresby. One bomb exploded less than 100 metres from their location, and a soldier changing his clothes dived hurriedly into a gutter near his tent. Minutes later there was an anguished yell, and a stark naked man streaked out of the gutter when large ants attacked various parts of his anatomy.

The general health of the 39th Battalion continued to be a problem. Constant heat and humidity turned minor scratches into nasty tropical ulcers, which often ate into shin bones. Dhobie itch was another irritating complaint, as it left 'red raw' rashes under the arms and crotch areas of the body. The threat of malaria was another constant threat.

On July 27th that year the inexperienced soldiers of the 39th Battalion began their arduous trek along the Kokoda Trail in the forbidding Owen Stanley Ranges. During their seven-day marathon walk, the young Diggers ascended and descended steep ranges, crossed treacherous rivers, stumbled over exposed tree roots, and sank into forest mulch, before they reached their first base camp.

The nervous novices first came under enemy fire on August 13th at Deniki, a small settlement which overlooks a section of the Kokoda Trail. George and his mates dropped quickly to the ground, but two members of the 39th were KIA, while another seven were wounded in that withering attack. Next day the remaining members of the unit commenced a strategic withdrawal, and they were forced to leave behind packs containing spare clothing.

By the end of the month the situation had become desperate for the 'Chocos'. On 29th July 1942 the 39th Battalion lost

"Chocos" on the Kokoda Trail

their commanding officer, when Lieutenant-Colonel William Owen was KIA by an enemy sniper. Major William Watson assumed temporary command, and the besieged Aussies withdrew down the track to the village of Isurava. There the undermanned Diggers lost ground when they came under siege once more, before Lieutenant-Colonel Ralph Honner became the new commander of the Battalion.

By then the under-nourished Aussies' clothes were permanently wet from constant rainstorms, and many were either injured or battling some form of tropical disease. Pulpy feet and respiratory complaints were common ailments. Their usual diet was bully beef and broken biscuits. Tentative attempts to cook rice were quickly abandoned, after smoke from cooking fires attracted a barrage of mountain gun fire and grenade attacks from the nearby enemy. 'Home was never like this', became a common phrase among the embattled Diggers, who became even more determined to 'make the Nips pay'.

On the 27th August 1942 a grim four day siege began at Isurava. Lieutenant-Colonel Honner realised that this was 'the last throw of the dice'. If the Isurava rest house fell before reinforcements arrived, then Port Moresby would be taken, and the Japanese would have effectively annexed New Guinea.

The next day, Warrant Officer George Cops led a group forward to the front line to recover the bodies of Corporal

George Anderson and Private Lionel Watts, who had been killed earlier that day. George felt the loss greatly after his comrades were buried, as he had been good friends with both Diggers.

However, on that day, the 2/14th Brigade arrived to provide back up support, and the presence of these fit and experienced soldiers lifted the spirits of the besieged 'Chocos'. On 29th August Private Bruce Kingsbury inspired his army mates, with a fearless attack on the advancing enemy. Kingsbury killed around 30 enemy soldiers, before a sniper took his life. This usually reserved hero was awarded a posthumous VC.

The now enlarged group of Australians continued to hold out the numerically superior enemy, and after the 25th Brigade joined them, approximately 550 determined 'Chocos' and 'Regs' defied the odds and kept nearly 5,000 highly rated Japanese soldiers at bay for four crucial days at Isurava. Lieutenant Colonel Honner later provided the following tribute to the sometimes maligned members of the 39th Battalion.

"In the testing crucible of conflict… they were transformed… by a burning resolve to stick by (their) mates."

Damien Parer, the renowned war photographer, also honoured the often under-valued contributions of Australian soldiers in New Guinea.

"…the Diggers have fought, and always will fight, for their cobbers: for 'Bluey' and 'Snowy', for 'Lofty' and 'Stumpy'."

Warrant Officer George Cops was guiding a platoon of 2/14th soldiers to an important vantage point, when the Japanese unexpectedly began to withdraw back down the

Kokoda Track.

The Aussies' own withdrawal to Eora Creek was difficult in the muddy and slippery conditions, and it was there where George buried Ernie Lingenburg, who was his mother's cousin. He had spoken to Ernie earlier that day, when a serious stomach wound was visibly taking its toll. After the war ended, his body was never recovered. Painful memories like that still linger in George's memory.

When Lieutenant-Colonel Ralph Honner congratulated the gallant members of the 39th Battalion at Menari, there were only 150 survivors remaining, from the original total of 700 active soldiers. George has never forgotten the six week ordeal on the Kokoda Track, where he learned to endure extreme hardship and stand up to a ruthless and skilful enemy. He was promoted to Warrant Officer Class 2 when he returned to Port Moresby, and later elevated to Class 1.

After serving as Regimental Sergeant-Major of a Machine Gun unit for 20 months, Warrant Officer Cops assumed that same position with the 9th Infantry Battalion at Madang, Alexis Haven and finally Bougainville, where he remained until the war's end.

Warrant Officer
George Cops

By then many horrendous scenes, which George had witnessed on 'the Track', took their toll, and he spent three months recuperating from a PTSD condition at the Australian General Hospital in the Bonegilla Army Camp near Wodonga. George gradually recovered his health, but to this day he regularly recalls distressing incidents from the ferocious battles which occurred on the Kokoda Trail.

Mateship with his army comrades sustained him during those desperate days, and it remains a vital part of the now 92-year-old's life. George still meets up with local mates at reunions, he corresponds regularly with interstate survivors, and he was a committee member of the 39th Brigade Association for 12 years after World War II ended.

George and his wife Una operated a grocery store in his home town of Beeac for 30 years after he returned to civilian life. The couple now reside in Ocean Grove, where George devotes much of his time making furniture for his family and friends. Both Una and he enjoy seeing their two sons, five grandchildren and six great-grandchildren on much treasured visits.

George found a much changed Papua New Guinea, when he returned to that country 25 years after the war ended. One of his sons worked in Japan for a few years, and George enjoyed the time he spent there during a holiday visit.

10

WORLD WAR 11 PROFILE: TED KENNA - THE HERO OF HAMILTON

Edward (Ted) Kenna was born in 1919 in the south western Victorian town of Hamilton. This esteemed war hero died in 2009, just two days after turning 90.

Ted was one of seven children, and during his boyhood years life was a struggle for the Kenna clan. His father died at an early age, and the family lived in a two-bedroom house which had no electricity. At times, if Ted and his brother Jack were unsuccessful on their after-school rabbit shooting excursions, the family missed out on their evening meal. Consequently, Ted became a deadly accurate marksman with his trusty 22 and 303 rifles, and this skill later served him well in armed combat situations.

Despite enduring rural poverty, Ted appeared to have a happy childhood. The Kenna's were a close-knit family unit, and seldom ventured far from home. In fact, Ted's first visit to Melbourne occurred when he was conscripted. Ted was educated at St. Mary's school in Hamilton, and he became an apprentice plumber, before he and brother Jack received their 'call ups' and became 'Chocos' in the army. Both were seconded to the 2/4 Battalion, and assigned to armed service duties in New Guinea.

On 15th May 1945, near the Wirui Mission at Wewak in New Guinea, Private Kenna's company was assigned the task of capturing enemy positions on a spur. The attacking sections were engaged by the enemy at close range, with heavy automatic fire coming from an undetected position. Casualties were suffered, and the attackers were unable to move forward. The situation was deteriorating rapidly until Private Ted Kenna, on his own initiative, stood up to obtain a better sighting of the hidden enemy. The Japanese snipers also revealed themselves, and opened fire on the brave Australian. One bullet grazed his chest, but all others miraculously missed. The little 26-year-old marksman from Hamilton continued to mow down the foe with unerring accuracy. At first Ted used a Bren gun in his attack, but he soon called for a more familiar 303 rifle when the Bren gun became too heavy and cumbersome.

Private Kenna killed many enemy soldiers on that fateful day, and no further injuries were sustained by the company once his audacious counter attack began.

Due to Kenna's magnificent bravery, in the face of concentrated fire, the bunker was captured without further loss, and crucial information was obtained on remaining enemy positions. Kenna's gallantry ensured his Battalion's success, and he was awarded a VC.

Two weeks later Ted Kenna received a serious rifle wound to the face, after he attempted to repeat the same strategy against another enemy unit. Ted believed that Lieutenant Whitehead saved his life that day, but the brave officer was unfortunately killed during the rescue.

After treating Ted's head wound, an army doctor rated his survival chances as being '60/40 against'. In fact, during early stages of his recovery, a priest anointed the young hero on at least three occasions, in preparation for his anticipated death.

It took another ten gruelling days of travel, before Private Kenna commenced treatment at the Heidelberg Repatriation Hospital in Melbourne, where he endured several operations over the next 12 months. During his rehabilitation, Ted was regularly cared for by an army nurse named Marjorie Rushbury. The couple fell in love, and they were married after Ted was discharged from the army in 1946.

Marjorie and Ted Kenna
at his VC award ceremony

Ted and Marjorie Kenna
on their wedding day

On 6th January 1947, Private Edward Kenna was awarded his Victoria Cross by the Duke of Gloucester, (who was then the Governor-General of Australia), at Government House in Melbourne.

The married couple raised four children after Ted returned to his home town, where he worked as a caretaker for the local council. Ted Kenna loved Hamilton, and he resided there until he retired from the work force. In his younger days he was an excellent bike rider and footballer. Ted's sporting highlight occurred in 1947, when he kicked the winning point on the day Hamilton won the local premiership.

Ted Kenna with Hamilton footballer teamates

During those years the council provided the Kenna family with a house, and a portrait of the town's major war hero, (painted by noted Australian artist, Sir William Dargie), is still displayed in the Hamilton Town Hall. In a nearby park, an impressive statue of Kenna VC can also be viewed.

Ted, Marjorie and their four children enjoyed overseas trips which honoured Victoria and George Cross winners. On one reunion excursion to the UK, Ted attended the 1953 Coronation of the young Queen Elizabeth. His family and he later met her, the Queen Mother and Prince Phillip, and they especially enjoyed regular trips with other celebrities to Norfolk Island. Sir Roden Cutler (VC), star Australian rock singer Normie Rowe, and World War II heroine,

Nancy Wake, sometimes accompanied the Kennas on these island reunions, where they stayed in a guest house owned by Colleen McCullough, the famous and recently deceased Australian novelist.

Marlene Day, who is Ted's youngest daughter, remembers that her mother greatly enjoyed these celebrity occasions, but feels her famous father was often ill at ease in public life situations.

Five VC winners (Partridge, Kenna, Hinton. Kelliher and Rattey at Edmonton(VC's) graveside in North Africa

In recent years, John Brumby, who was Victoria's premier between 2007 and 2010, requested a meeting with the ailing Ted. The Premier had family connections in Hamilton, and when he arrived at Marlene and Ian Day's Drysdale home to meet up with the war hero, he brought a bag of lamingtons with him, as his contribution for morning tea.

During his time with Marlene and Ian, the usually reticent Ted Kenna participated in a candid radio interview. He had previously spoken little about his war experiences to family and friends, so it was an illuminating experience to hear the VC winner's thoughts about war.

"Just dirty war… that's all it is. Nothing is worth war… it won't heal anything."

He expressed the same sentiments at a Victory Parade in Melbourne.

"I hope there's no more war for our kids," was his comment at that gala occasion.

In the home-based interview, Ted revealed that his main dread in combat situations was the fear of letting his army mates down, as well as misgivings about his reactions in potential crisis situations.

Ted's main wartime regret is the memory of mates like Lieutenant Whitehead, who

Ted Kenna at Victory Parade

never returned from combat. Subconsciously, memories of his lost mates remained.

"In the back of your skull, (it's there) all the time," he confided in the interview.

To Ted, the strong spirit of mateship among Australian service personnel was not a myth. While the mateship concept is difficult to explain outside a war situation, it remains a lifelong influence, among those who share the possibility of imminent death in combat zones.

His VC citation states that Private Kenna 'displayed the highest degree of bravery' at Wewak on 15th May 1945, but

Ted modestly dismissed any assertion that his actions were heroic,

"Just a job...Just doing my job," was his laconic assessment.

Ted Kenna also revealed his dry sense of humour in the interview. His long marriage to Marjorie was obviously a great and enduring love story, but the impish war veteran could not resist remarking that, while nursing him at Heidelberg,

"She trapped me on my death bed!"

Two years after Ted Kenna's death, Marlene and Ian Day added their own insightful observations about his character and personality. Both agree that 'taking on' the armed Japanese soldiers at Wewak, was typical of the man they knew. Ted Kenna was always a competitive, determined and stubborn man, but he met his match when he opposed Sir Donald Bradman in a deck quoits competition on board the 'Orcades' on a 1968 voyage to England. The two Australian heroes engaged in a long and spirited struggle, before the cricket great finally triumphed.

Ted Kenna never stood on ceremony and treated all people the same.

"We'll beat you Pommies in cricket again," was one alleged comment he made to Queen Elizabeth II.

Ted Kenna (VC) with the "Orcades'" ship captain

Daughter Marlene summed up her father's character in the following way

"He was very pragmatic and optimistic, and not one to dwell on problems…He was also modest and loyal, and lived for his family, grandchildren and great grand-children."

In his later years, Ted Kenna continued to stoically accept whatever circumstances fate decreed him. He regretted leaving his home in Hamilton, but adjusted to life in Drysdale with Marlene and Ian, before relocating to a Grovedale nursing home in nearby Geelong. Around that time Ted became more physically vulnerable. He suffered a heart attack, he became a diabetic, and, after breaking his hip in a fall, Ted Kenna was confined to a bed until his death.

Perhaps it was his love of a challenge which saw Ted Kenna soldier on until the age of 90. He died two days after reaching that milestone.

"That might do," was Ted's alleged comment, two days before his death. An 84 year-old Marjorie passed away six weeks later.

Ted Kenna's only regret focussed on his grandchildren and great grandchildren because he

"Wouldn't be there for the little ones."

11

WOMEN IN THE WAR FRONT

"They become lost souls. They (the armed forces), take them away. They break them, and then give them back to us."

These revealing observations were provided by an anonymous war widow. They accurately mirror the ongoing anxieties, tensions, and at times physical dangers, which many wives, mothers, sweethearts and children endure in their shared lives with physically or mentally scarred war veterans. These family members cope with the bouts of insomnia, repetitive nightmares, depression, abrupt mood swings and alcoholic rages, from a man who has become damaged and dangerous.

Eighty-nine year-old Marie McIvor experienced two markedly different types of post-war behaviour, after her father and husband both returned home from the Great War.

She recalls that her father's personality changed significantly.

"(My) mother said before (my father) went to the war he was a nice happy type of person, and when he came back he was an atheist and had a sort of chip on his shoulder."

In contrast, her husband, Simon McIvor, saw every day as being a 'bonus' when his wartime service with the RAN ended, despite losing a lung after his ship was wrecked by bombs. McIvor's prognosis was so poor that the navy enquired where the family would like him to be buried, but the patient lived.

"He survived pretty well," said Marie. **" War didn't affect my husband's outlook on life, because he had a nice, happy nature. (His attitude was) whatever happened yesterday is gone."**

Initially Marie was hesitant about marrying a man who was 27 years her senior, but they enjoyed a happy relationship until he died from pneumonia in 1967.

Today, in her Brisbane residence, Marie McIvor has little time for war.

"It's a waste of young lives, an absolute waste."

It appears that soldiers on active duty are not the only casualties of war. A 19 year-old Albert ('Bert') Robert Shirley was assigned to the 44th Infantry Battalion in 1917, but contracted pulmonary tuberculosis after arriving in England, and was banned from active service.

Today his daughter, Sue Barker, believes her late father gradually developed 'survivor's guilt'. The unhappy and restless man married and divorced twice, and he developed a serious dependence on alcohol. Bert's lifestyle fortunately became more settled after he married Evelyn Barness. The couple reared five children when they lived at Kalgoorlie and Albany. Bert Shirley seldom mentioned his past problems and he was 81 when he died in 1979. His grave in Albany's Allambie Park Cemetery overlooks the harbour where the first Anzac convoy of ships gathered, before sailing on to Gallipoli.

"Why is your face so white, mother?
Why do you choke for death?
Oh I have dreamt in the night, my son
That I doomed a man to death."

(Extract from a popular World War I anti- conscription song).

Amelia and Charles Martin felt both grieved and guilty, after their son James ('Jim') Martin died from enteric fever off Gallipoli in October 1915. The lad should never have been allowed near any battle-front, as Jim Martin was only 14 when he perished. The well-built youngster from rural Victoria looked 18 years of age in his physical appearance, and when his 42-year-old father was rejected for war service on medical grounds, his son vowed to take his place. In fact, Jim Martin threatened to abandon the family home forever, unless his parents lied about his age and gave him written permission to enlist.

Amelia apparently believed that authorities would soon discover Jim's true age and expel him from the forces, but this did not eventuate. When Jim Martin passed away at the age of 14 years and nine months, he became the youngest ever Australian to die in active service. Marriage relations between the guilt ridden parents may then have then become strained, for the couple separated eight years after their son died.

Historically, the roles of women on the home-front in times of war have been greatly underrated. When men are engaged in military service, it is the wives or mothers who accept responsibility for raising children and managing household budgets. Ongoing concerns for their partner or son produces a stressful environment. Furthermore, if their men die on far away battlefields, the women folk sometimes grieve alone.

Olwyn Green chose to become an author as part of her own grief therapy, after her husband Lieutenant-Colonel Charles ('Charlie') Hercules Green, was KIA during the Korean War. Green was a legendary leader of the 3AR Regiment in Korea. Previously, at the age of 25, Charlie Green became Australia's youngest appointed Commander, when he led the 2/11 Battalion during World War II campaigns in New Guinea.

Olwyn Green

Following Green's tragic death, Olwyn was left a war widow with one child. She later documented her husband's life in a book titled *The Name's Still Charlie*.

*

During World War 1, opportunities arose for women to involve themselves in worthwhile fund raising activities. Organizations such as The Australian Red Cross, the Country Women's Association, (CWA), the Christian Temperance Society, the Australian Women's National League, the Voluntary Aid Detachment, the Australian Comfort Fund and the Cheer Up Society, all assisted in supporting the war effort on the home front. Involvement in these activities was both socially and emotionally rewarding.

Some of these groups, or more modern counterparts, functioned effectively in World War II. The Women's Land Army originated during that conflict, and adult females worked in farm labouring roles, which had been assigned to men in pre-war years. One famous member of the Land Army was the aboriginal activist, Faith Bandler AC, who was 96 when she died on 13th February 2015.

Faith Bandler

Doris Johnson and Marjorie Johnson, ('the first Mrs J'), met in this war-time club, when they shared duties on a farm near Tallarook in Victoria. The two became close friends, while Marjorie Johnson's husband served overseas. Marjorie later died at the age of 43, and two years later Doris married the widowed husband, (who was older than her by 26 years).

Major Neville Johnson served in both World War I and World War II. In the former conflict he enlisted as a 20-year-old with the Australian Army Medical Corps, and he later drove a horse – led ambulance with the 3rd Light Horse Brigade in the Middle East.

In his written memoirs Johnson recalled seeing screaming limbless soldiers, while others suffered serious scalp injuries. Major Johnson seldom spoke about these horrific experiences. He was discharged with a heart condition in 1917, and Doris and he settled near Euroa in north-east Victoria. Neville Johnson was 82 when he died in 1979. His resilient 91-year-old widow is reportedly still alive, and she now resides in a Euroa nursing home.

Many more women joined the work force during World War II, sometimes in factories or in other occupations which had previously only been undertaken by men.

Other women committed themselves to front-line battle ground roles, a scenario which first began in the Boer War. Volunteer female nurses and teachers served in South Africa, and 2,000 women in the Australian Army Nursing Service, (AANS), were involved in World War I action. During the Gallipoli campaign, many of these nurses were based at the nearby Greek island of Lemnos, where they initially attended to soldiers who had suffered only minor injuries.

Matron Grace Wilson arrived on this windswept barren island with 96 other nurses, shortly after the 1915 August offensive was launched 60 kilometres away at Gallipoli. Initially their Casualty Clearing Station (CCS) was virtually non-existent. When a bagpiper welcomed

Matron Grace Wilson

them to the island there was no hospital, no supplies, little water and few stretchers. Nurses ripped up their petticoats to provide make-shift bandages, and attended to wounded soldiers lying on the rocky ground. Flies, scorpions and centipedes continually made life difficult, dysentery became a huge problem because of the poor sanitation, and more soldiers were being treated for diseases than for war wounds.

The advent of winter introduced frostbite and gangrene to their 'island from hell'. Nurses were forced to work

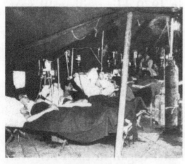

shifts lasting at least 16 hours. Hurricane lanterns provided the only form of medical lighting available, and the three operating tables at their disposal were used 24 hours a day. At one stage on Lemnos there were reportedly only seven

World War 1 hospital

nurses on hand to care for nearly 560 patients. Despite such hardships, the approximate casualty rate on the island among injured soldiers was only 2%.

The actual number of World War I nursing volunteers was likely to be close to 5,000, as many others made their own way to various theatres of war. The Bluebirds, (so named because of their noticeably blue coloured uniforms), was one of these groups. About 20 nurses joined this team, which was organised by the Red Cross and financed by the Australian Jockey Club.

Helen Wallace was one of the Bluebirds, and her granddaughter, Linden Wilkinson, is currently campaigning for the Bluebirds, and similar nursing groups, to be given official recognition for their World War I service.

Ms Wilkinson remembers her grandmother as a mostly stoic woman, except when an aeroplane flew over her Sydney home. The haunting memory of the sound of planes in combat zones never left the World War I nursing war veteran: she would hide under the kitchen table until the aircraft had flown by.

The same motivating influences which activated their male counterparts encouraged women to volunteer for overseas service.

Olive King

Olive King probably sought adventure when she became an ambulance driver in France and the Balkans during World War I. In that role King saved a countless number of lives, for which she was decorated by a grateful Serbian government.

Later Olive King helped to establish a string of canteens to help feed displaced Serbian people.

After returning to Sydney Olive first became State Secretary of the Girl Guide's Association, and for the decade between 1932 and 1942, she was State Commissioner of that organisation. Olive King was 73 when she passed away.

Vera Deakin was the youngest daughter of former Prime Minister Alfred Deakin. This determined woman overcame her parents' concerns, and became actively involved in World War I welfare work. She founded a Wounded and Missing Persons Bureau in Cairo and later in London.

In 1920 Vera Deakin married Thomas White, who was later knighted. Vera also remained active in public life. She became Life Governor of the Royal Children's Hospital, and in 1945 she was made a Life Member of the Red Cross.

Vera White was survived by a daughter, when she died at the age 87 in 1978.

On 22nd July 1917, four young nurses became the first Australian women to receive war bravery awards. On that night the 2nd Australian Casualty Station at Trois Arbres near Armentieres in France was bombed by German aircraft. All four women were on duty, and they ignored patients' pleas to find shelter from the bombing raids. After the station was plunged into darkness, Nurse Alice Ross-King was injured when she fell into a bomb crater. Later she provided a graphic diary account about the mayhem which surrounded her.

Alice Ross-King

"Though I shouted, nobody answered me, or I could hear

nothing for the roaring of the planes. I seemed to be the only living thing about...I kept calling for Wilson, (a medical orderly), to help me... but the poor boy had been blown to bits."

Later she, as well as nurses Claire Deacon, Dorothy Cawood and Mary Derrer, each received a Military Medal, (MM) for rescuing patients from burning buildings.

Alice Ross-King married Sydney Theodore Appleford, when she returned to civilian life. She and her doctor husband settled in Victoria's South Gippsland area, and the couple raised four children.

When World War II began, Alice Appleford enlisted with the Voluntary Aid Detachments, (VADs), and she later became a Major in the renamed Australian Army Women's Medical Services.

In 1949 Major Appleford was awarded the Florence Nightingale Medal by the International Red Cross.

She was 77 when she died in 1968.

Dorothy Cawood served on various other war sites in Europe, before returning to Sydney in May 1919. She later became Matron at the David Berry Hospital, and died at Parramatta in 1962.

Claire Deacon was discharged in March 1919. Three years later she married a dentist named James McGregor in a Melbourne registry office. Claire McGregor was 61 when she died from meningitis in 1952.

Nurse Rachael Pratt was recommended for a MM when she was serving on the island of Lemnos near the Gallipoli invasion point. Despite suffering a punctured lung from shrapnel wounds, Nurse Pratt continued her care of injured soldiers until she collapsed and was removed from the action.

She undertook a long period of recuperation, and suffered from severe bronchitis for the remainder of her life.

At the end of World War I, Rachael Pratt returned to Melbourne where she became a partner in an East Malvern rest home. She was 80 when she died at the Heidelberg Repatriation Hospital.

In July 1917 Elizabeth Pearl Corkhill also received a MM, for displaying conspicuous bravery during a bombing attack at Longvillers on the Somme. Her calmness under pressure lifted the morale of injured soldiers in her care.

After the war ended, Pearl Corkhill held various nursing positions in private hospitals, and for the decade between 1951 and 1961 she was a Senior Sister at the Bega District Hospital on the NSW South Coast.

In retirement at Akolele, Pearl Corkhill was often an MC at local functions, and she was also a fine horsewoman. She was 98 when she died.

The community minded women described above, all appeared to have exhibited conservative and predictable values in their post-war environments. They were productive women, and circumstantial evidence suggests that the mental effects of war zone experiences had minimal effects on their quality of life.

Nancy Wake was also a war hero, but this controversial and adventurous woman was markedly different in the lifestyle she chose to follow.

She is currently Australia's most famous war heroine. By 1943 Nancy Wake had become so effective as a spy, saboteur and resistance fighter, that she topped the German Gestapo's most wanted list.

Previously she had endured a dysfunctional childhood.

Nancy was born in a dilapidated shack in Wellington New Zealand, and was the youngest of six children. The teenage girl was devastated when the father she dearly loved never returned from America to the Sydney family home. At the age of 16 she 'fled the nest' and worked, (under an assumed name), for two years as a nurse in Mudgee.

Nancy Wake

Fortunately, an unexpected bequest from a New Zealand aunt then enabled Nancy Wake to travel to England, where she became a journalist. At the time, the Nazi Party was becoming prominent in pre-World War II Germany, and Nancy vehemently opposed their Fascist propaganda.

In 1936 she met French millionaire Henri Fiocca and the couple married shortly after World War II began.

Nancy then became a courier for the local French Resistance movement, and she carried vital messages and equipment to other partisans. In her role, the attractive young woman would openly flirt with the German soldiers, if it assisted her plans.

Before long Nancy Wake was taking groups of refugees, grounded Allied pilots and Jewish families from one 'safe house' to another. As her fame spread, the Gestapo dubbed Nancy 'the white mouse' because of her ability to avoid capture.

Her French husband, Henri, was not as fortunate. After being captured by the Gestapo he refused to reveal Nancy's whereabouts, and was consequently executed.

"I will go to my grave regretting that," Nancy later lamented.

"…Henri was the love of my life."

Following Henri's death, a 16 week training course in London with the Special Operations Executive further honed her explosives, weaponry and hand to hand combat skills. Nancy Wake then became a skilled operator behind enemy lines.

On 31st March 1943 Wake was parachuted back into an area strong in partisan support. Her goal was to accommodate the leaders' munitions needs, but she soon realised that these 'macho' men did not respect the foreign female in their midst. A few drinking bouts, at the end of which Nancy Wake was the last 'man' standing, resulted in her capabilities becoming more respected.

On one raid, Nancy Wake allegedly killed an SS sentry by slitting his throat. Her life then revolved around ambushing German soldiers, blowing up bridges and wrecking trains.

Her French partisan groups soon gained notable victories. Vichy was liberated from Marshall Petain's collaborationist groups, and Wake became one of the first Resistance leaders to enter Paris, when the German dominance began to crumble.

Later, at the Paris based British Officer's Club, 'the white mouse' became 'the mouse which roared' after a haughty waiter declared that he would rather serve German customers than her boisterous revellers.

Nancy immediately leapt to her feet and knocked the waiter senseless with a vicious right hook. Furthermore, when a concerned colleague brought the stunned waiter a brandy, it was the Australian Resistance leader who skulled the offered drink, before vacating the premises.

Nancy Wake received many honours for her outstanding war-time feats, including the American Congressional Medal of Freedom, the George Medal from Britain, and the Legion d'Honneur, the Croix de Guerre and the Medaille de Resistance from France. Controversially however, five decades elapsed before an Australian government offered her a medal.

Nancy Wake

The premise underpinning this strange decision was simple: Nancy Wake had never actually fought with Australian Armed Services during World War II. Finally, when government figures belatedly approached her, Wake emphatically rejected the opportunity to accept an Australian award. Eventually, in 2004, she was made a Companion of the Order of Australia.

At first, Wake struggled to adjust to civilian life once World War II ended. She re-married, but after husband John Forward died in 1997, she relocated to Britain. Nancy Wake was 98 when she died on 7th August, 2011.

In the twilight of her days, noted Australian author, Peter FitzSimons, compiled her colourful life story. During one interview she confided her burial wishes.

"I want to be cremated, and I want my ashes to be scattered over the mountains where I fought with the Resistance. That will be good enough for me."

All the women profiled above in this chapter, managed to survive wars, unlike the 71 females who lost their lives in World War II action. Forty-one of these servicewomen were nurses serving in the Pacific war, and many of those deaths took place in an infamous massacre inflicted by Japanese soldiers on Banka Island. South Australian nurse Vivian Bullwinkel was the only one who survived the mass executions.

Previously, in early February 1942, Vivian Bullwinkel, and 64 other AIF nurses were sailing on a small coastal steamer named 'Vyner Brooke', before it was badly bombed by Japanese planes. Twelve nurses drowned or were shot dead after all on board abandoned ship. Other exhausted survivors spent up to 60 hours in the sea before reaching Banka Island. Unfortunately they then elected to surrender to the Japanese, who had recently landed on that remote outpost.

Firstly, the enemy forces separated the 23 male captives and took them away from the main group. Shortly afterwards, the sound of shouts and sustained gunfire was heard. None of the captured men came back, and the returning Japanese soldiers had blood stains on their bayonets and clothing.

The 22 surviving nurses were then ordered to wade into the water off Muntok Beach, where all but one was massacred from behind by the soldiers on shore.

Sister Vivian Bullwinkel was the last in the line of nurses. She was the tallest one present, and the Tommy gun fire, which fatally penetrated the bodies of her colleagues, struck her in the side and shoulder. Fortunately, while Bullwinkel lay still in the shallow water, the Japanese soldiers rushed off to intercept another of load of shipwrecked troops who had landed further up the beach. Miraculously Vivian Bullwinkel survived, and she later re-lived her terrifying experience in a diary entry.

"I saw the girls fall one after another...Then I was hit.

It (the bullet), missed all the organs... Later I took myself into the jungle... I knew what happened to everyone else... I did find a tin of condensed milk, but I had no way of opening it."

For a few days Bullwinkel and a stranded male sailor called Kingsley, survived on supplies provided by villagers. Shortly after his 39th birthday the other fugitive died, and Bullwinkle was again forced to surrender to the Japanese. During her long period of detention she did not allude to the massacre for fear of reprisals.

All the nurse captives were given the option of becoming 'comfort women' or prostitutes for the enemy soldiers. After that offer was rejected, they were housed in poor quarters where little food was provided and sanitation was virtually non-existent. Four more Australian nurses died after they were housed in even worse conditions in Sumatra, and diseases such as malaria, beriberi and dysentery became rife.

Agnes ('Betty') Jeffrey was another captive nurse, who later wrote about her POW experience in a book titled *White Coolies*. Sister Harper and she spent three days in water and mangrove swamps, and they also survived on a fisherman's raft for a short time before they were captured.

In her book, Betty Jeffrey describes how she and the other starving women in the Sumatra prison camp managed to survive.

"We find we can eat most of the grass growing near the creek; also the young growing ferns with sweet potato are like eating mushrooms."

By August 1944 the war was

Agnes ('Betty') Jeffrey

nearing an end, but the starving nurses' situation remained diabolical. The overworked and under nourished women were denied essential medicines and Red Cross parcels, and their cruel Japanese custodians would not allow them to write letters. Consequently there was no communication with their families at home for at least 18 months.

Despite their privations the plucky nurses managed to preserve their dignity, and the close friendships they developed with their fellow inmates helped them to cope and adapt to their prison life.

Australian authorities remained unaware of their plight after the Japanese surrendered on 15th August 1945, until Australian war correspondent Hayden Leonard found 24 emaciated survivors living in primitive conditions at Loebok Linggau.

They arrived safely in Darwin a month later, after enduring three years and seven months of gruelling privation. Sister Betty Jeffrey, who was then very ill with tuberculosis, only weighed 30 kilograms, while most of Sister Bullwinkel's hair had fallen out. Later, when Vivian Bullwinkel gave evidence in Japan at a war trial, she became obviously traumatised after hearing once more the language and accents of her former captors.

Lieutenant Colonel Vivian Bullwinkel

Lieutenant-Colonel Vivian Bullwinkel later became Director of Nursing at Fairfield Hospital in Melbourne. In September 1977 she married Colonel Francis West Statham, and in 1992 Vivian Statham returned to Banka Island, where she unveiled a memorial plaque which honoured the massacred nurses.

Lieutenant Betty Jeffrey spent nearly two years recovering in hospital, after returning from her internment. She later became a nursing administrator in Melbourne, and was affectionately remembered for her infectious sense of humour.

The two women went on to publicise their war experiences, both at home and abroad, and lived long lives before they passed away in the year 2000. Vivian Statham, (MBE, AM), was then 84, while Betty Jeffrey, (OAM), died at the age of 92.

On 14th May 1943, the Australian Hospital Ship 'Centaur' was sunk by a Japanese submarine south of Moreton Island off the Queensland coast. The ship was clearly marked as a hospital vessel, and on the night this war crime occurred these markings were illuminated by bright floodlights. Three hundred and thirty-two mostly sick and wounded passengers were on board, and only 64 survived this barbaric assault.

The surprise attack began around 4 a.m. when a torpedo struck a fuel tank on the ship's port side. The tank burst into flames, there was a huge explosion, the bridge super structure collapsed, and the funnel crashed onto the deck. A blazing fire swept rapidly through the ship, which sank in a matter of minutes.

Many were either killed in the explosion or drowned. Several volunteers from the Australian Medical Corps were included among the dead, as were 11 women from the Australian Army Nursing Service.

Sister Ellen ('Nell') Savage was the sole survivor of the nursing staff on board. She did sustain severe bruising, a fractured nose, burst ear drums, a broken palate and fractured

Sister Ellen Savage

ribs. However this strong swimmer was able to access a makeshift raft, to which other survivors were clinging.

There Nell Savage became an inspiration. She persuaded the group to participate in prayers, rosary recitations and community singing, which helped them cope with the fact that visible rescue vessels were unknowingly passing them by. Finally, after drifting for 36 hours, the exhausted survivors were rescued by USS 'Mugford'. Shortly after, Sister Ellen Savage's strong leadership qualities were recognised, as she became only the second Australian woman to be awarded a George Cross.

After the war Nell Savage became the Senior Sister at the (Royal) Newcastle Hospital, and in 1947 she took up a Florence Nightingale scholarship in England. On her return to Australia in 1950 she accepted the position of Matron at Rankin Park Hospital.

Nell Savage was 72 when she died on 25th April 1985. She, along with Vivian Bullwinkel and Betty Jeffery, appeared to overcome horrific war zone experiences, and adapted well to civilian life.

12

MATESHIP IN WAR ZONES

"We never lost our spirit, even if we lost our strength."

Facts bear out Betty Jeffrey's bold assertion. Some of the POWs captured with her after the Banka Island massacre, composed a song titled *Song of Survival*. Thirty Australian, Dutch and British women prisoners shared their lipsticks and 'best' clothes, before presenting this song and other musical items at well-attended POW concerts. The performers on stage mostly stayed seated, as they were too physically weak to stand. These popular concerts were regularly staged throughout 1944, even though half of the original performers died during that same year.

Sport also helped to build mateship and improve morale in various enemy POW camps. During World War II the inmates of Stalag 344 near Munich became preoccupied with planning escapes, frustrating their captors, receiving letters and Red Cross parcels from home, and playing sport. Building escape tunnels was a priority which sometimes clashed with game commitments, and on one occasion a star player was absent for an important game. It was rumoured that 'he was in the tunnel'.

A variety of sports was played on their small and grassless parade ground, including cricket, soccer, rugby and softball.

There was even a surf life-saving club at Stalag 344.

Cricket games began at 8 a.m., and play was possible until at least 9 p.m., because of the long European summer twilights. After play ended for the day, spirited discussions about the state of the game would continue on into the night. Consequently cricket and other ball sports became important diversions from the monotony and strains of prison camp life.

Flair and initiative was displayed in producing equipment for matches. Wounded soldiers spent much of their time making matting surfaces from Red Cross bags, and the Red Cross and YMCA later provided other cricket gear for the POW camps. Large, parochial crowds of nearly 3,000 people provided strong support for English, Australian, New Zealand and South African 'Test' teams, and gambling on matches was common. Cigarettes were usually the currency for wagers, and sometimes Red Cross parcels were gambled on results. Umpires wore white coats borrowed from the camp hospital, and most German guards would willingly retrieve balls which landed in out-of-bounds areas.

William H. Walker was a strong supporter of the English team, and when the 'Poms' lost a vital 'Stashes Ashes Test' match against Australia, he penned the following obituary which closely resembled the original Ashes message.

"In affectionate remembrance of English wartime cricket, which died in Stalag 344 on 6th July 1944. Deeply lamented by a large group of POWs of all ranks. R.I.P.

N.B. The body will be cremated, and sent to England with the next repats."

Cartoon illustrations presented here, are copies of the originals which were created by a Stalag 344 artist.

"My mind goes back to '43, to slavery and hate
When one man's chance to stay alive,
depended on his mate...
You'd slip and slither through the mud,
And curse your rotten fate,
But then you'd hear a quiet word.
'Don't drop your bundle, mate."

(Poet unknown)

Sport was also a wonderful diversion for World War II inmates of the notorious Changi POW camp in Singapore. Against all odds, a six-team AFL type competition was organised. Wilfred ('Chicken') Smallhorn, a brilliant Fitzroy wingman, who previously won

Wilfred Smallhorn

a prestigious Brownlow medal in 1933, was one of the main organisers.

The Changi league had approximately 200 registered players, two appointed umpires, and a tribunal which handed down fines and suspensions for any serious player misdemeanours. Movement of footballers between teams was allowed, and three bowls of rice was usually considered to be a reasonable transfer fee. Inmates carved out their football ground from thick jungle within the prison walls. The best and fairest player for the season was awarded the Changi Medal, which was reportedly made from a segment of a crashed Japanese aeroplane.

"They teach you how to shoot and kill,
You learn which enemy to hate;
But nowhere in their training do you learn
How to deal with the loss of a mate."

(Tribute poem by Vietnam veteran, Lachlan Irvine)

Ernest James ('Ernie') Brough, (MM) was confronted by some extremely gruesome encounters during World War II. Near El Alamein, in the Western Desert campaign, he was once assigned the grim task of identifying several army mates who had been dead for days.

Later, in the early weeks of 1943, he witnessed the brutal and unnecessary execution of a fellow inmate by the Italian commandant of Camp 57, near the village of Gruppigano in the Italian Alps. Ernie and 3,000 other prisoners endured the unpredictable sadism of that commanding officer for seven stressful months.

Ernie remained sane by playing chess, maintaining a small

carrot garden, and dressing up in style for a 'race' day, where no horses were available for prisoners to punt on.

The inmates also played an improvised form of baseball. The 'ball' used in games was actually a suitably sized rock, which had been wrapped tightly in twine. Games were very competitive between Ernie and his army mates.

Mateship is often associated with Australian service personnel, though it is not unique to our military culture. However, for at least two centuries, Australian politicians of all parties have lauded the tradition of Australian mateship.

Australian PM's-John Howard and Julia Gillard

In 1999, Liberal Prime Minister John Howard insisted that 'mateship' was a hallowed Australian word, and on Australia Day 2011, Labor Prime Minister Julia Gillard asserted that 'Mateship defines our nation'. For a country which currently tends to be dismissive about spiritual beliefs, mateship at times appears to almost be a de facto form of religion, and an essential part of our national identity. This behavioural trait seems to be especially strong within Australian armed services.

Mateship between Diggers transcends the boundaries of normal friendships, and even marriage vows. Furthermore,

Private Bill Jackson

it is not essential for service people to personally enjoy the company of all their army, navy or air-force mates.

However, when a group bond is strongly forged in potentially dangerous combat situations, each individual knows that he or she can depend on their combat mates to look after their welfare in life and death scenarios. In battle zones, expectations of endurance, courage, loyalty and a willingness to sacrifice everything for your fellow comrade in arms, all fall under the mateship umbrella.

Late at night on 25th June 1916, near Armentieres in France, one badly wounded Aussie soldier fortunately found a true mate in Private Bill Jackson. Bill grittily overcame severe pain caused by a serious shoulder injury, and carried his more seriously wounded comrade through heavy fire to safety. By then Private Jackson's arm was nearly severed from his shoulder, and it later had to be amputated. His brave action was recognised with a VC award.

Over a year later, in July 1917, a public function was held in the NSW town of Hay to welcome home Sergeant Cambden and Private Jackson. Cambden spoke emotionally about Jackson's valour, and informed the gathering that

"Bill was not looking for a VC that night. He was looking for a cobber."

Lieutenant Frank Hubert McNamara was an officer with Unit 1 Squadron Australian Flying Corps during World War I. On 20th March 1917, the squadron was involved in a raid on Tel el Hesi in Palestine. Captain David Rutherford, who was involved in the same operation, was unfortunately forced to land his damaged plane behind enemy lines. Lieutenant McNamara was seriously wounded in the same mission, but he came to Rutherford's rescue after he saw a Turkish cavalry group galloping towards his stranded and injured mate.

Lieutenant Frank Hubert McNamara

However the now incapacitated rescuer failed to make a safe landing and his plane crashed and turned over in a nearby gully. Fortunately, after McNamara crawled out of his wrecked plane, Rutherford managed to re-start his own aeroplane. McNamara's revolver fire, together with armed assistance from two other pilots, managed to halt the Turks' charge. The two pilots soon became airborne again, and flew to a nearby safe base.

McNamara later proved to be a reticent and modest hero and claimed that he was

"An ordinary man, thrust into the limelight by one truly amazing episode."

Following the dramatic escape, Lieutenant McNamara nearly died during his recuperation period in hospital, after suffering an allergic reaction to a tetanus injection. He was later appointed Acting Air Vice-Marshall of the RAF, but became an embittered man after being made redundant by the RAAF. In later years Frank McNamara relocated to England, and in 1961 he died in Buckingham at the age of 67. He was survived by a wife and two children.

*

"Your mate alongside you became your mother, father and God all rolled into one."

(Sergeant 'Bunny' Pulfer, who was KIA at Isaruva)

Private Richard Kelleher was a soldier with the 2/25th Battalion, which came under heavy fire near Nazab in New Guinea on 13th September, 1943. In the attack, Commander ('Billy') Richards and two others were wounded, and another five were killed.

Kelleher adamantly declared that he was going to save Commander Richards. He rushed the nearby enemy post, and hurled two grenades into the Japanese ranks. He then returned with a Bren gun and silenced the enemy gun-post, before braving enemy fire and rescuing his wounded section leader. His courageous actions saved a fellow Digger, and resulted in Private Kelleher receiving a VC.

The Irish born Kelleher's health was badly affected by constant malaria attacks in civilian life. He worked as a gardener in Melbourne until his death at the age of 53. Richard Kelleher was survived by his widow, who later re-married.

Private Francis John ('Frank') Partridge was attached to the 8th Battalion, which became involved in significant action on New Guinea's Bonis Peninsula on 25th July 1945.

Private Partridge received wounds to his left arm and thigh when the group was fired upon by Japanese soldiers, but he ignored the dangers around him and retrieved a Bren gun from a dead comrade. This weapon provided cover fire for Partridge, when he launched a successful grenade attack on an enemy bunker. He then killed a Japanese soldier with his knife, before blood loss from his serious wounds caused him to temporarily abandon his attempt to take over another enemy bunker. The still badly injured Partridge later returned to the action, before his platoon was driven back by the numerically superior enemy. His heroic deeds were honoured with a VC award.

When the conflict ended, Frank Partridge returned to the family farm near Macksville in NSW. There the seemingly confirmed bachelor lived with his father in a dirt-floored house. At night Frank would light up the kerosene lantern, and read volumes of the Encyclopedia Britannica.

His studies revealed that Frank Partridge possessed an amazing photographic memory, and he became a highly successful contestant in the hugely popular general knowledge program *Pick a Box* on national television. Viewers warmed to his laconic personality in his entertaining duels with the previously incomparable Barry Jones, and Frank Partridge became one of only three contestants to pick all 40 of the contested boxes.

Partridge was well rewarded financially for his general knowledge prowess, and in 1963 he unexpectedly married a 31-year-old Sydney nurse. Partridge also unsuccessfully attempted to gain Country Party pre-selection for the Federal seat of Cowper in that same year.

In 1964 Frank Partridge was unfortunately killed in a car accident. He was only 39, and left a widow and three-month old child.

*

Corporal Reginald Roy Rattey was attached to the 25th Battalion, which became involved in a ferocious battle near Buin Road in South Bougainville on 22nd March, 1945.

In a fearless solo effort, Rattey used a Bren gun and grenades to rout an active enemy gun post. Despite being under heavy fire, Corporal Rattey returned to his base to replenish his grenade supply, and then routed another Japanese gun post. His single-handed assaults brought success to his unit in less than an hour, and Corporal Rattey's gallant performance was rewarded with a VC.

At the end of the Pacific War, Reg Rattey returned to West Wyalong, where he became a soldier settler. Rattey's first marriage produced one child, and after being widowed he remarried and fathered another four children.

After ending his farming career, Reg Rattey captured tiger snakes for the Gosford Reptile Park, and he also worked as a commercial fisherman. Rattey was 68 when he died, and he received a full military funeral in his home town.

Corporal John ('Jack') Hurst Edmondson was born in Wagga Wagga, but moved to Liverpool near Sydney, where he worked on his parents' farm before enlisting for war service.

Corporal John Edmondson

Jack Edmondson was a member of a seven-man team with the 17th Battalion, which sought to turn back a German advancement at Tobruk on 13th April 1941. Though seriously wounded, the plucky Edmondson ignored the heavy fire around him, and continued to advance on the foe. He killed three Germans, and saved the life of his platoon leader, Lieutenant Austin Mackell.

The German attack was defeated, but Edmondson died of his wounds shortly afterwards.

The 26-year-old corporal was awarded a posthumous VC for the bravery he displayed, and today a commemorative clock in Liverpool honours the heroic deeds of Corporal Jack Edmondson.

Warrant Officer Class 11, Kevin Arthur ('Dasher') Wheatley, was assigned to three companies on a tour of duty to Quang Ngai Province in South Vietnam. On 13th July 1965, Wheatley, and fellow Warrant Officer R.W. Swanton, were in charge of a group of soldiers on a search and destroy mission. Swanton received life threatening chest wounds when the group came under heavy fire. Consequently Wheatley made a radio request for Swanton to be air lifted from the danger area, and for an air strike to be launched on the enemy.

Such actions were not immediately possible, and Wheatley was instructed to abandon his seriously injured mate and return to a safe position. This order was ignored. Instead Wheatley discarded his heavy radio equipment, and half-dragged and half-carried the wounded Swanton through heavy fire from an open rice field to a safer wooded area.

Once more Wheatley was urged to leave his badly wounded comrade and escape from the danger area, and again the advice was ignored. When the advancing Viet Cong troops circled to within ten metres

Kevin Arthur ('Dasher') Wheatley

of the defiant Digger, Wheatley was last seen with two live grenades in his hands.

Next morning the two Australians' shot bodies were discovered. Twenty-eight-year-old Warrant Officer Class 11 Wheatley, who chose certain death in order to protect a mate, was awarded a posthumous VC.

Dasher Wheatley was one of life's battlers, who was only 17 when he married his 14-year-old sweetheart. Wheatley worked in various labouring jobs until he entered army ranks at the age of 19, and he gained a reputation of being tough and wild during his service years in Malaysia. Wheatley's nickname originated from his rugby union background.

Warrant Officer Kevin Arthur 'Dasher' Wheatley was survived by his widow, Edna, and their four children.

Warrant Officer Class 1 Keith Payne, (VC, OAM) fortunately survived a similar situation in the Vietnam War. Payne was commanding the 212th Company of the Mobile Strike Force Battalion in Kontum Province on 24th May 1969, when they were attacked by a large North Vietnamese unit. The Australians faltered under intense fire, but Payne, despite suffering hand, arm and hip wounds, kept the enemy at bay

with his Armalite rifle and grenade counter attack.

After assisting in a planned withdrawal from the danger area, Warrant Officer Payne returned to the combat zone that night. While under heavy enemy fire, he located approximately 40 Aussie soldiers who had previously been isolated from the main group. Payne

Keith Payne

organised the rescue of many of his comrades, and personally dragged and carried some of the more seriously injured to safety.

Keith Payne was awarded a VC for his brave life-saving actions. He gradually recovered from his own injuries in his home state of Queensland, and today this father of five sons is a valued spokesperson for the war veteran community in Australia.

*

America's and Australia's military involvement in Afghanistan had its roots in a terrorist attack on 11th September 2001. In that massacre on mainland America, which was perpetrated by 19 suicide Muslim extremists, nearly 3,000 innocent members of the public died in four separate attacks on New York, Washington DC and Pennsylvania. George W. Bush, the then President of U.S.A., immediately issued this grim warning to the perpetrators.

"We will make no distinction between the terrorists who committed these acts, and those who harbour them."

Afghanistan had the reputation for being a safe haven for enemies of the West. Consequently, when it was strongly rumoured that Osama bin Laden, (the suspected master-mind behind the September 11 attacks), was hiding in remote areas of the mountainous country, America quickly landed military forces in

President George W. Bush

that often inaccessible part of the world. It was an invasion which was never sanctioned by the UN Security Council.

Australia's then Prime Minister, John Howard, was supportive of our ally's robust stance, especially following the public outrage which erupted throughout our nation after 12th October, 2002. On that dreadful day, in the Indonesian resort town of Bali, 88 Australians were listed among the 202 victims, who were exterminated by massive explosives ignited by South-East Asian Muslim extremists. International terrorism was seen as a threat to all, and defending ourselves and fellow Australians against violence at home or aboard, became an essential priority.

Initially in Afghanistan, Australian Special Task Force Squadrons in Afghanistan were deployed in military operations against Taliban insurgents.

This fanatical Muslim fundamentalist group supported Bin Laden's al Qaeda terrorists, and opposed the democratically elected government of their own country. In early stages of the conflict, Australian Diggers featured prominently in the capture of Kandahar airport. Later, between August

Osama Bin Laden

2006 and 2013 the main focus of attention was limiting the influence of the Taliban in Uruzgan Province.

It was a frustrating and formidable challenge. Forty Australian servicemen were KIA during the war in Afghanistan, and seven of the slain Aussies were 'green on blue' executions. This term describes the insidious practice of mentored and supposedly loyal

Afghan soldiers murdering the Australians, who were training them to safe-guard their own country.

The 'jury is still out' about the long-term success of Australia's counterinsurgency strategies in Uruzgan Province. Australia hopes that productive changes they instigated in the agricultural heartland of Afghanistan will reduce the risk of Taliban dominance across the country.

During the occupation period Colonel Paul Burns served as Australia's SAS Commander. The following conclusions were later part of his review process.

"It's about the people wanting an alternative future... which in my mind is free from Taliban intimidation. It's not us who are going to win the fight; it's going to be them... Our role was to provide that buffer to remove the Taliban leaders."

Trooper Mark Gregor Strang Donaldson is one of four current Australian servicemen who have been awarded VCs in the Afghanistan war. On 2nd September 2008, Trooper Donaldson was a member of Special Operations Task Force 'Operation Slipper' in Uruzgan Province, when this multi-national group was ambushed by a large number of Taliban soldiers.

The allies were subjected to fierce machine gun and rocket fire which inflicted heavy casualties, and their advance was halted. During the early stages of the conflict, Trooper Donaldson reacted decisively to revive his group. He moved rapidly between alternative positions of cover, while engaging the enemy in

Mark Donaldson

gun battles. Donaldson even deliberately exposed himself to the view of Taliban marksmen to draw fire, so wounded mates could be rescued and returned safely to convoy vehicles.

When the trucks were filled with injured comrades, Donaldson and other uninjured allied soldiers experienced heavy fire from the enemy as they ran alongside the retreating convoy. Mark Donaldson noticed a severely wounded Coalition Force Interpreter lying helplessly on the open ground 80 metres from safety. He was dangerously exposed to Taliban attacks. The sandy haired Australian abandoned the forced withdrawal and rushed to his foreign mate's side. He dragged him through heavy enemy fire to safety.

After successfully applying first aid to the Interpreter and other other injured soldiers in the convoy, Mark Donaldson returned to the raging gun battle. His heroic efforts were later described as being

"Conspicuous acts of gallantry, in circumstances of great peril".

Twenty-nine-year-old Trooper Mark Donaldson became the first Australian serviceman to receive a VC award in nearly 40 years.

Corporal Benjamin Roberts-Smith was a Patrol Second-In-Command of a Special Operational Task Force engaged in another 'Operation Slipper' assignment, during a helicopter assault into Kandahar on 11th June 2010.

After arriving in their 'chopper', the group was subjected to heavy machine gun fire from multiple positions. Two of the Task Force suffered wounds, and the remainder of the group was pinned down by continual fire from three machine gun positions in elevated and fortified positions.

Corporal Roberts-Smith bravely reacted by moving under

heavy fire to within 40 metres of an entrenched Taliban position.

In a close-quarter encounter he killed an enemy insurgent, before drawing fire away from his group by fearlessly exposing his position. This decoy tactic enabled his Patrol Commander to silence a machine gun post with a successful grenade attack. Corporal Roberts-Smith then stormed another machine gun post, and killed the two remaining gunners.

Corporal Ben
Roberts-Smith

These courageous and inspiring actions released his patrol from intense fire, and caused a serious invasion of the enemy position. The village of Tizak, and the Shah Wali Kot Province, were consequently cleared of Taliban insurgents.

Previously, on his second tour of this war weary country, Ben Roberts-Smith was awarded a Medal Of Gallantry, (MG). Then, following his 2010 heroics, Corporal Benjamin Roberts-Smith was honoured with a VC.

This 36-year-old 'man mountain', (Ben Roberts-Smith is around 200 centimetres in height), originates from a high achieving Perth Family. His father, Len, headed the Western Australian Occupation and Crimes Commission, and his brother Daniel is a talented opera singer. Ben Roberts-Smith is a married man with twin daughters. Recently he resigned from the army, and is now employed in a civilian position.

In August 2010, Corporal Daniel Keighran was attached to the 6th Battalion of the Royal Australian Regiment in the village of Derapetin, which is located in the Tangi Valley region of Afghanistan. There, in a combat situation, he exposed himself to enemy fire on many occasions, which drew fire away from his Digger mates. Crucially, he also provided target information for his Regiment's 25 mm gun crews, who were manning three Light Armoured Vehicles on higher ground.

During the three-hour battle, Corporal Keighran showed little regard for his personal safety, and he was awarded a VC for his brave actions.

The modest 31-yearold is now married to his childhood sweetheart Katherine. Before leaving army life, Keighran was a strong advocate for Diggers suffering mental health problems. He developed much empathy for those less fortunate, after experiencing an underprivileged childhood in outback Queensland.

Dan Keighran is now a shift worker at the Frog's Leg Gold Mine in Kalgoorlie.

*

"All I remember is just being numb… not sad…or angry… just sort of numb."

(An Australian soldier in Afghanistan, after losing a mate in battle).

Commando Corporal Cameron Baird became the 100th Australian to be awarded a VC, after he posthumously achieved that honour for his conspicuous acts of bravery in the Khod Valley of Uruzgan Province, on 22nd June 2013.

By then the strongly-built Cameron Baird was already a highly respected and fearless warrior from the Sydney based 2nd Commando Regiment. During the fatal encounter, Corporal

Baird made three attempts to overwhelm heavily fortified enemy soldiers defending mud huts. In each involvement he endeavoured to draw fire away from his Digger mates, so the group could achieve its combat objectives.

Cameron Baird received the fatal shots after kicking down the door of a hut.

Corporal
Cameron Baird

*

**"Weep for the waste of all that might have been,
Weep for the cost that war has made obscene,
Weep for the homes that ache with human pain,
Weep that we ever sanction war again."**

(*Honour the Dead-* words written by Shirley Erena Murray, music composed by Colin Gibson)

Chaplains have been associated with wars for many years, and during World War I Walter Dexter became a legendary figure in the cult of mateship, after he established appropriate and respectful burials for Diggers killed on the battle fields of Gallipoli and the Western Front.

Trooper Dexter originally fought in the Boer War, and after becoming an ordained Anglican minister, he served as an Army Chaplain in Gallipoli and later in France. This 'man of great gifts' established a well patronised coffee stall at Becourt Wood in the Western Front campaign, but Dexter's care for the dead was his greatest contribution.

Prior to his intervention, corpses would be exposed to the elements wherever they perished. The stench from their rotting bodies was so appalling that both the Turks and Anzacs agreed to a day-long armistice. In those hours of peace, the landscape was cleared of dead bodies and cherished slain comrades were respectfully buried.

The insightful Chaplain also logged and mapped the location of wartime graves, so that the families and loved ones of fallen Diggers could properly pay their future respects. In his final days at Gallipoli, the legendary man of God scattered silver wattle seeds around the graves, which he dedicated to future generations of Australians.

"I intend to leave a bit of Australia here", was Walter Dexter's diary explanation.

He later became a minister at various Victorian parishes, and all five of his sons volunteered for military service in World War II. Walter Dexter (DCM, DSO, MC) was 77 when he passed away in 1950. He left a widow and six children.

"At the going down of the sun, and in the morning, We will remember them."

(*For the Fallen*, a poem by Laurence Binyon)

Another 'larger than life' religious adviser during World War I, was Army Chaplain William ('Bill')McKenzie, (OBE). Bill was the son of a Presbyterian Scot, who cultivated a cane farm near Bundaberg after emigrating from his homeland. Spiritually his son was drawn to the Salvation Army at a young age. He joined their ranks, and married a woman from that persuasion in 1899.

Bill McKenzie became an Army Chaplain in 1914 with

the 4th Battalion. This huge man was soon dubbed 'Fighting Mac'. At Gallipoli he won the respect of even the most hardened Digger with his readiness to tend to the wounded and the dead. McKenzie was the man every Digger wanted tomeet. His popularity continued when he served on the Western Front, where his booming voice was often heard in song.

Bill McKenzie

However by 1917 Bill McKenzie was a broken man.

"I have seen so many fine chaps killed…I have buried so many…Is it worthwhile living?"

After being awarded a Military Cross, (MC), Bill McKenzie was released from military service. Over 7,000 people welcomed him home, when he returned to Melbourne in early 1918. He later served the Salvation Army in northern China, and became a high ranking clergyman with the Army before his death in 1939.

Father Norbert ('Nobby') Earl was serving his congregation of over two thousand New Guineans at the Sacred Heart Mission near Samurai in East Papua, when he was forced to evacuate to the relative safety of Port Moresby during World War II. He became an Australian Army Chaplain in order to stay in that war torn country, and was attached to the now famous 39th Battalion.

Father Earl projected a sense of calmness and goodness to the hardened Diggers, and he won their unconditional respect near the tiny village of Pirivi on the Kokoda Trail. There, when a dead Digger lay in 'no man's land' while both combatant groups were under heavy fire, Father Nobby stood up and advanced calmly towards the dead soldier with spade in hand. Unexpected silence fell over the scene, as all firing ceased while the Chaplain prayed over the body. He then reverently dug a hole and buried the slain warrior. Father Nobby was then allowed to return safely to the 39th Battalion before hostilities resumed.

*

At times an unusual type of personal mateship appears to transfer across enemy lines. At Gallipoli in World War I, and at Tobruk in World War II, ceasefires were mutually agreed to, so that both sides could take a meal break, or attend to burials for their dead colleagues. In those much appreciated moments of peace, cigarettes, food and halting conversations were sometimes exchanged between rival camps, before savage armed hostilities were resumed.

"I am the enemy you killed, my friend
I knew you in this dark;
For so you frowned yesterday through me
As you jabbed and killed..."

This stanza of verse is taken from Wilfred Owen's acclaimed poem titled *Strange Meeting*. In his poem, Owen imagines a disturbing but respectful post life meeting with a German soldier he has previously killed. It mirrors at least two authentic war time encounters, which occurred on the Western Front in World War I, and near El Alamein during World War II.

In March 1917, at Lagnicourt in France, Captain Percy Cherry from Tasmania engaged in a gun battle with a lone German soldier. Both men were seriously wounded in the encounter, but the dying German managed to pass on some of his personal letters to his Australian assailant. Days later, when Cherry finally recuperated from his own gun battle wounds, he honoured his word to the slain enemy and posted off the German's correspondence. Sadly, in that same month, Captain Percy Cherry, (VC) was KIA.

Captain Percy Cherry

An even more dramatic example of mateship between enemies occurred in the Western Desert during World War II.

Between 23rd October and 2nd November 1942 at El Alamein, Warrant Officer Ernie Brough became involved in a successful foray against General Rommel's troops. Ernie captured six enemy prisoners, before discovering another German with a seriously injured right foot. The lean Aussie was faced with a dangerous dilemma. He could either take the new prisoner to his own camp, which was approximately 300 metres away, or carry him to where the Germans had a large hospital tent, about 400 metres from where they were located.

Remarkably it was the more hazardous option which Ernie Brough chose. The laconic Australian hoisted the wounded man onto his back, picked up his small camera to record the action, and started to advance towards the German camp. At first explosions from a heavy gunfire attack, blew Ernie off his feet, but the unlikely warrior mates soldiered on. Thankfully, as they drew nearer, the Germans ceased fire, and Ernie Brough was able to return the wounded soldier to the safe haven of his own camp.

The respectful Germans did not fire a single shot at Ernie when he walked back to his own base, and the now 94 – year-old Captain Ernest Brough, (MM) wonders (a) What became of the anonymous foe whose life he saved? and (b) Did anyone ever find the camera he dropped during that daring and successful rescue mission?

Rats of Tobruk - Artie Byens (Dec) and Ernie Brough (MM)

13

THOSE MAGNIFICENT MEN IN THEIR FRAGILE MACHINES

"The aeroplanes are wonderful. Great squadrons of them are often in the sky- 20 or 30 of them humming like huge bees far above us... Air fights (create) great excitement."

(A World War I observation from Corporal Alan Jukes)

Aviation made its armed combat debut during World War I. The first operational aeroplanes soon became a vital resource for reconnaissance and mapping purposes and for observing enemy troop movements.

The challenge of flight was very much in its infancy. It was less than a decade since the Wright brothers from America had successfully launched an air borne machine above the ground for an historical few minutes.

Consequently, when these flimsy machines made their first appearances in war zones, life for these 'knights of the air' was incredibly hazardous. Construction designs for planes were both flimsy and dangerous, with canvas being attached to wood for the framework of the machine. Only small bombs could be carried on the planes and machine guns on board would frequently jam on dangerous battle missions. Early air skirmishes saw pilots optimistically throwing grenades at the enemy, and air crews would dangle grappling hooks out of their planes in mostly fruitless attempts to snag the propellers of enemy air craft.

Navigation relied on map reading skills and observing landmarks on the ground below – as long as the cloud cover was not too thick. Initially senior commanders forbade the carrying of parachutes on board, as they were too heavy and might negate the fighting spirit of pilots. Only day time missions were possible throughout World War I.

Overall planes were so unsafe, that at least 50% of pilots lost their lives in training exercises before they ever became involved in combat flights. Little wonder that pilots who flew these flimsy machines appeared to be reincarnations of Errol Flynn and Keith Miller, in their cavalier approach to life.

During the World War I years, the Australian Flying Corps (AFC) squadron was connected to the Australian Infantry Forces, (AIF), which was attached to the larger British Royal Flying Corps. Approximately 3,700 men served with the AFC, and 175 World War I airmen lost their lives in that form of service.

The Royal Australian Air Force, (RAAF), was not established until 1921, so World War I Australian war pilots and flight crews served with Britain's Royal Air Force (RAF).

The most successful World War I Australian flying ace was Flight Commander Robert Alexander Little, (DSO and Bar, DSC and Bar), who was born in the Melbourne suburb of Hawthorn.

Little learned to fly at his own expense in England, and his air combat ability was considered to be superior to his aviation skills. He

Robert Alexander Little

survived a number of crash landings in his brilliant but short lived aviation career, but he had a keen eye, and was 'the epitome of deadliness' with his revolver or rifle in close up combat encounters.

Flight Commander Little gained an impressive 38 victories (or hits to enemy aircraft) in less than a year. He was then rested from air combat for six months, and scored another nine 'hits' on enemy aircraft after returning to active duty. Unfortunately he was KIA at the age of 22. A widow and young son survived this 'gentle, resolute and kind man', who became Australia's most prolific World War I strike pilot.

Squadron Leader Roderick Stanley (Stan) Dallas, (DSO, DSC and Bar), was a former mining truck driver from Esk in North Queensland.

Stan Dallas obtained 39 flight victories, and he also became a much respected squadron leader and test pilot. This flying ace had a casual attitude about claiming victories, but his leadership qualities and rapport with combat mates was excellent. Stan Dallas was elevated to the rank of Lieutenant Colonel, but this 26-year-old air base humourist of note was KIA over France in June 1918.

Significantly more Australian airmen became 'knights of the sky' in World War II, with air crews involved in combats over Europe, North Africa, Burma, New Guinea, Australia and the vast waterways of the Indian, Pacific and Mediterranean regions.

By late 1944 the RAAF had 182,000 personnel, 61 squadrons and 6,200 aircraft, and within a year it had become the world's fourth largest aviation service. When World War II ended nearly 10,000 of our airmen had paid the supreme sacrifice, and more than half of these fatalities occurred over Europe. Now, in the early years of the 21st century, the Australian air force participates more in joint operations with our army, navy and international allies.

Clive Robertson ('Killer') Caldwell, (DFC and Bar), was Australia's most successful flying ace in World War II. He was credited with 20.5 victories. Originally he was a war recruit who was too old to enlist, but Caldwell altered his birth certificate in order to gain acceptance.

'Killer', (a nickname he disliked), graduated as a Pilot Officer in the Empire Air Training scheme, which operated in Australia, Canada, Zimbabwe, (formerly Rhodesia), and Britain during the war. This veteran of the skies participated in 250 missions, and the majority of his combat flights were over Syria, Palestine and North Africa.

Clive Caldwel

Flight Lieutenant Paterson (Pat) Hughes (DFC) was the youngest of 12 children born to a Cooma school teacher. Pat Hughes later graduated from the RAAF, and joined the RAF for war-time service. He then became 'the real driving force' behind the RAF's 234 Squadron, and became renowned for his daring close-up battle skills against enemy aircraft.

In 1940 Pat Hughes met his future English wife Kay. She was tragically widowed after five weeks of marriage, when her 22-year-old husband became one of 24 Australian airmen who perished in the Battle of Britain.

Flight Sergeant Rawdon ("Ron") Hume Middleton was a member of a RAAF Unit attached to No 149 Squadron, which became involved in a bombing raid over Italy, between 28th and 29th November 1942.

Middleton was participating in his 29th mission, so he was then one short of compulsorily ending his tour of duty. On this final exercise, Flight Sergeant Middleton was captaining a Stirling BF 472 on an air-raid attack which was targeting the Fiat factory in Turin.

Middleton was making a third identification flight over the Italian city, before the windscreen of his aeroplane was suddenly shattered when it was struck by anti-aircraft fire from below.

Both his co-pilot and he were badly wounded in the attack. Middleton's right eye was severely damaged by a shell splinter, and his jaw was broken. This caused him to momentarily lose

Rawdon Middleton

consciousness, and the plane initially suddenly dropped 250 metres. Fortunately the second pilot righted the machine, and the bombs were still released over the target.

The now conscious Middleton ensured that his co-pilot received first aid, before returning the battered plane safely to England. The blood covered Middleton experienced much pain, but he was obviously 'there for his mates'.

"I'll make the English coast, I'll get you home," the gallant leader kept repeating over the intercom.

When they finally reached the English Channel only a few minutes of fuel remained, so Middleton ordered his crew to parachute out of the plane. Five of the crew obeyed his instructions and landed safely, but the flight engineer and flight gunner stayed on board. They then attempted to persuade Middleton to make a crash landing in England. This suggestion was rejected by Middleton, as they would have landed somewhere in a residential area. Consequently, he turned back over the water. The two remaining airmen parachuted into the English Channel, where they unfortunately failed to survive. Middleton crash landed into the sea after his fuel supplies ran out, and two days later his body was recovered on a beach near Dover.

Ron Middleton was Sydney-born, and he was a great nephew of the famous explorer Hamilton Hume. Prior to the war he worked as a jackeroo on his father's NSW property, and he was 26 when he was KIA.

Keith William ('Bluey') Truscott (DFC and Bar), became the second highest World War II flying ace, after he was credited with achieving 20 confirmed and five unconfirmed victories. Truscott was born in the Melbourne suburb of Prahran, and between 1937 and 1940 he played 44 games of VFL football with the Melbourne club. Truscott was not highly rated as a pilot, but he was a daring and skilful fighter in air combat. He became a flight commander and acting squadron leader, and was noticeably prominent in missions off Milne Bay during the New Guinea

Keith ('Bluey') Truscott

campaign. Truscott was later killed in a flying accident after being transferred to Darwin.

John Lloyd Waddy (OBE, DFC) was the son of Edward Lloyd Waddy, a NSW state cricketer. John Waddy became a successful war pilot, who claimed 15 victories in the North African desert campaign, with four of these 'kills' being claimed in the one mission. Waddy later commanded number 88 Squadron in the South-West Pacific war zone, where he gained a US Air Medal. John Waddy later became a NSW parliamentarian, after he returned to civilian life.

Keith Ross Miller, (AM, MBE), is still probably the finest all-round cricketer to ever represent Australia. During World War II Miller piloted aircraft over battle zones of Germany and the North Sea, with the same nonchalant daring that he displayed in Test match cricket.

Sir Michael Parkinson, the

Keith Miller

legendary television interviewer, once asked Miller about the pressures which international cricketers faced. The handsome Australian laughingly replied

"Pressure? There's no pressure. Having a Messerschmitt flying up your arse is pressure, cricket is not!"

Test cricket was never more than an enjoyable game for this incorrigible and charismatic dare-devil, who always lived life to the full. In January 1942 the 22-year-old, Keith Miller interrupted his promising cricket career, and enlisted in the RAAF. After attending flight training classes in Australia, Miller undertook advanced training in England with the RAF. He gained experience flying Beauforts, Beau Fighters and DH Mosquitos, and survived some scary encounters.

Miller was once forced to land while a displaced bomb was still dangling under the plane. Fortunately the bomb did not explode.

In another incident, Flying Sergeant Miller reported a fault in his plane's mechanism after making a dangerous forced landing. The defect was supposedly repaired, but on its very next flight another pilot was killed when the plane crashed.

Between April and May of 1942, Keith Miller was assigned to No. 169 Squadron which assisted allied air operations over Europe. Targets included German V-1 and V-2 production and test launch sites on North Sea islands, as well as a military installation in Denmark.

On one mission Miller broke away from his flying formation, and returned to base later than other members of the squadron. This lover of classical music had taken 'time out' to fly over the city of Salzburg, where the famous German composer, Wolfgang Mozart, was born.

The laconic and abrasive Australian frequently faced insubordination charges from superior officers. On one occasion a dishonourable discharge was even considered, after Keith Ross Miller was found guilty of being drunk and disorderly. Allegedly all was forgiven when he agreed to play cricket with the investigating officer's team.

Keith Miller

After representing Australia in 55 Test cricket matches, Keith Miller retired from the game. He then became a journalist, a sports commentator, an advertising celebrity, a public relations officer and the owner of some slow racehorses, before dying at the age of 85 in 2004.

*

"Not for us some old-time glorious death, no regimental camaraderie
As each alone in darkness holds his breath,
While enemy coast below blots out the sea...
Then, coned in light at twenty thousand feet,
The land below a mass of burning fire."

Cecil Edgar Robertson ('Boz') Parsons was born in the Victorian town of Colac in 1918. His father, Cecil Edgar Parsons, (who possibly provided the lifelong nickname of 'Boz' for his son after a character in a Dickens' book), died at a young age. Boz was only seven when his mother Lena Parsons, and her six children, re-located to Geelong.

Lena Parsons was an enterprising woman who provided

a private school education for all her children. Boz obtained a scholarship to Geelong Grammar, from where he matriculated, and in 1939 he graduated in Science from Melbourne University.

By then Boz Parsons had a strong desire to fly aeroplanes. This long lasting ambition, combined with a sense of duty to the British Empire, motivated him to enlist in the Australian Air Force for World War 11 duties.

Boz was accepted into the Empire Air Training Scheme, which saw him travel initially to Canada to continue his pilot education training, before completing his course in England.

An excited Boz Parsons started as a second pilot with Bomber Command in RAF number 58 Squadron, and his plane had a crew of five. The first missions were mainly observational for the inexperienced Australian. On one night attack Boz remembers trying to follow a target map, which he was reading upside down, while using the brightness of probing enemy search lights to follow instructions.

Boz Parsons

Boz participated in seven Bomber Command operations as a second pilot and 18 as a captain in his 25 missions over various parts of

Germany. Initially the main problems encountered were climatic, with strong winds, icy windscreens on foggy nights, and the non-existence of radar equipment, often producing inaccurate bombing raids.

He still vividly recalls being caught in the cone of enemy searchlights thousands of feet above the earth.

"It was a very unnerving experience... You feel completely naked... you're sitting up there, and you don't feel as if you are moving."

Inevitably, following the atomic bomb obliterations of Japanese cities Nagasaki and Hiroshima, questions were asked about the morality of wartime bombing attacks of civilian targets. Boz once asked another pilot how he felt about "what was going on underneath you?" He received a pragmatic answer.

"I didn't feel at all. I just wanted to get home."

In general, Boz Parsons agreed with these sentiments, and added that

"I think that was a realistic attitude. To be perfectly truthful, you are more concerned about surviving, if you are being shot at up there at 20,000 feet, you're not really thinking about what's underneath...it would be terrible if it was on your mind all the time...War produces a totally different state of mind...You're in something which is barbaric-you are on one side or the other."

Overall Boz Parsons considers he led a charmed life during World War II. There were no fatal accidents in locations where he was training, and his aircrafts were never seriously damaged by anti-aircraft fire.

He did, however, lose a lot of good friends. In fact, only 12 out of 24 men he initially trained with in Australia returned home at the end of the war. Among the personnel serving Bomber Command, the casualty rate was nearly 50%.

There is no doubt that the RAF became crucial in the Allies' final victory. Huge amounts of German military resources were needed in air combat, which would otherwise been deployed against Russia and D-Day invasions from the west. A former Nazi leader summed up the situation with these comments:

"The air war opened up a second front long before the invasion of Europe. The front was over the skies of Germany. The unpredictability of these attacks, made the front gigantic...Defence against air attacks required the production of thousands of anti-aircraft guns, the stockpiling of tremendous quantities of ammunition all over the country, and holding in readiness hundreds of thousands of soldiers... for months at a time....This was the greatest lost battle on the German side. The losses from the retreats in Russia or from the surrender of Stalingrad were considerably less."

Boz Parsons also served in the Pacific War between 1944 and 1945, flying B 24 Liberators out of Darwin. At first he flew with the Americans of the 380th bombing group, and later with the RAAF Liberator Squadron no. 24 against targets in northern New Guinea and the Dutch East Indies, (now Indonesia). At the conclusion of the war Flight Lieutenant Cecil Parsons was awarded a DFC.

In civilian life, Boz first became a commercial pilot, and was based in Alice Springs. He and his new wife, Barbara, then became share farmers at Ardrossan in South Australia. In 1962 he began what proved to be a highly successful teaching career at his former school, Geelong Grammar, where he mostly taught agricultural science and chemistry. Boz was a respected teacher and popular house master for 18 years, before he retired in 1980.

This amazingly resilient man continued to fly light aeroplanes around various parts of Australia until he was 94. Now, in his 96th year, this former war veteran, farmer and educator, still regularly plays golf at the Barwon Heads club.

Barbara and Boz raised three children. His eldest son, Bill, became an Air-Force pilot for a decade, before joining Cathay Pacific in 1980, and flying Boeing 747's out of Hong Kong for 25 years.

"Oh I have slipped the surly bonds of Earth,
Danced the skies on laughter silvered wings…
And done a hundred things you have not dreamed of.
I've chased the shouting wind along and flung
My craft through footless halls of air.
I've topped the wind-swept heights with easy grace,
And…put out my hand, and touched the hand of God."
(John Gillespie Magee)

Allan McKenzie McDonald junior was born in the Victorian town of Winchelsea on 21st August 1923. His father, (Allan McKenzie McDonald Sr.), was a World War I veteran who saw action on the Western Front at Bullecourt and Polygon Wood, before being repatriated back to Australia. Allan McKenzie senior then entered politics, and was the state Member for the seat of Polwarth, before becoming the Federal Member for Corangamite. This popular politician in the Menzies government served as the Minister for External Territories.

McDonald was also the Parliamentary whip, before he died from cancer in 1953.

Allan McKenzie Jr. was educated at the Winchelsea State School and Geelong College, before he left school at the age of 15, and began working with Dalgety's Farmers Ltd. When World War II began Allan McDonald followed his father's example and enlisted in the armed forces.

His son, Barry McDonald, later became the third generation of the family to serve in the armed forces, when he joined the Engineers Corps in the Australian Army. Originally Barry hoped to replicate the examples of his father and grandfather, but lazy eye problems ended his ambition to gain acceptance with the RAAF. Instead, Barry McDonald enlisted in the army, where he reached the rank of Major before retiring to civilian life.

Allan McDonald Jr. believes his father was motivated by a sense of duty to the British Empire, when he volunteered his World War I services. His son was swayed more by a sense of adventure and peer group pressure, and he was originally drafted into the army before being allowed to switch his allegiances to Air Force duties.

Allan McDonald Jr. then became involved in the Empire Air Training Scheme, and completed a course at bases in Somers, Benalla, Deniliquin and Mt Gambier.

In 1943 he travelled to the UK, where he honed his skills as a Navigator Bomb Aimer at Operational Training Units, (OTUs), in Scotland and Yorkshire, before joining a group of English airmen in Bomber Command Squadron 158. Previously he had trained with Whitley aeroplanes, but he preferred the British Hercules Mark 2 planes, which he worked with at Riccall base in Yorkshire.

Allan McDonald spent a year with Bomber Command, and today the now 91-year-old veteran has nostalgic memories of his three year stint in Britain with the RAF. The excitement factor associated with flying 19 night and 18 daylight missions was exhilarating, and he still treasures the camaraderie which existed among crew members, even though only two are still living. Allan also met his English sweetheart during those golden years. The couple married in England when the war concluded, and the union remains strong after 69 years of marriage.

Allan's third mission over Duisburg was dangerous but ultimately rewarding. On the day-time attack, anti-aircraft fire from below struck their plane and destroyed a motor. Their propeller began to rotate at an alarming rate, before separating from its mountings, and crashing into the aircraft. Despite this setback, the plane still dropped its supply of bombs, and flew slowly at low levels in freezing conditions to the safety of their English base.

Then the crew was unexpectedly summoned back to Duisburg that very night. On this mission they bombed the enemy city so heavily that flames appeared to engulf the entire area.

Allan McDonald Jr. made a smooth transition to civilian life after returning to Australia. He returned to Dalgety's where he became stock manager for Western Victoria. For the final 20 years of his working life he was employed by H.F. Richardson's Real Estate and Livestock in Geelong. He is now a proud father, grandfather and great-grandfather, and spends much of his leisure time at the Barwon Heads Golf Club.

Ernest (Ernie) George Truman was born in the

Melbourne suburb of Yarraville in 1921, and, after obtaining his Intermediate Certificate, became a clerk at the Newport Railway workshop.

His late uncle had been killed in the Great War, and Ernie faced spirited opposition from his mother when he volunteered for World War II duties with the RAAF.

At that stage England had a chronic shortage of airmen to operate their growing fleet of war planes. Consequently the Empire Training Scheme was introduced, which fast-tracked the training of personnel in Zimbabwe, Canada and Australia.

Ernie Truman completed most of his training in Australia, and became qualified as a Sergeant Observer from the Benalla campus in Victoria. Later, when he became part of a seven-man operational crew in England, Ernie Truman was assigned the role of Navigational Bomb Aimer.

Six Aussies and a native of Yorkshire made up the crew.

British Prime Minister, Winston Churchill, held high hopes for the RAF, and on 3rd September 1940, he famously predicted that

"The navy can lose the war, but only the Air Force can win it."

In early stages of the war, Britain's war leaders appeared too optimistic, as bombing results were disappointing, with only about 4% of missiles impacting on designated targets. Fortunately, a marked improvement occurred in the strike rate, and soon large areas of German industrial cities in the Ruhr Valley were reduced to rubble from concerted bombing attacks. The morale of the enemy consequently plummeted.

There was also a high casualty rate in the RAF, with thousands of airmen being KIA. It is a matter of record, that only 40% of air crews survived a tour of 30 operations.

Warrant Officer Truman was attached to Squadron 460, and his team of seven was assigned to bomb Mersburg where an important oil refinery was located. The Australian Bomb Aimer and Navigator still vividly remember how frightening the war zone was at night. Far below them many miles of countryside were ablaze, probing search lights turned night into day, and deafening explosions shook the attacking Bomber Command planes, which hovered over target areas like gigantic insects.

Squadron 460 achieved only minimal success on its initial raids, so a few nights later more attacks were mounted. The search lights were so bright on that occasion that Ernie Truman 'could have read the Herald'. This was a more successful mission, and Warrant Officer Truman was satisfied with his 'good hits'.

Duren, with an estimated population of 45,000, was another challenging mission. Allied intelligence sources discovered that a German Panzer Division had assembled there, near a major rail junction. A vital supply train was expected to arrive soon, and Ernie's squadron, (protected by a group of fighter planes), mounted a daylight bombing raid. Thick cloud cover resulted in the squadron flying as low as 10,000 feet above the ground, but Bomber Command was delighted with the success of the mission.

Ernie also recalls the massive raid which Squadron 460 launched over Nuremberg. Four five hundred pound petrol bombs, with long delay fuses were loaded onto his plane, and when the bombing assignment was over the whole city appeared to be on fire.

Disaster struck in January 1945 when Warrant Officer

Truman's crew was shot down by a German Junkers 88 night fighter aircraft. His highly respected pilot and two gunners perished in the attack, while Truman, and the other three surviving crew members, parachuted into enemy territory. Ernie lost a boot after landing in the snow covered terrain, but he managed to hide himself in a pine forest. Soon Ernie lost all feeling in his injured leg, so he surrendered himself to an elderly German couple, who notified authorities.

Ernie then became a POW in a camp outside Nuremberg. About 150 prisoners, mostly from Britain and America, were detained there, and rations were scarce for the inmates. Warrant Officer Truman lost about eight kilograms in weight during his imprisonment.

When advancing Russian forces drew near, German authorities surprisingly chose to move the POWs to another location, and in early April 1945 the prisoner evacuation began. It was stipulated that only one Red Cross parcel was allowed between every two prisoners each week.

By then battle-front casualties for both combatants continued to be horrendous. In late March 1944, Bomber Command lost 95 aircraft in raids over Nuremberg, and more than 30 planes were badly damaged. It was reported that more airmen were lost in just one raid than in the more famous Battle of Britain.

In 1945 Ernie Truman's parents were initially informed that their son was missing in action. Then, three months later, the relieved couple found that he was in a POW camp. The angst may well have taken its toll on Ernie's father, who died shortly afterwards. Ernie still believes that authorities could have been more efficient and sensitive with their information procedures.

Today an energetic 93-year-old Ernie Truman still lives life to the full. He is involved in his local RSL Sub Branch, Men's Shed and Probus clubs, and he purchased a new car after he turned 90. In 2012, Ernie Truman flew to England where he joined other Bomber Command veterans at a celebration reunion.

Overall the airmen profiled above, appear to have been less traumatised by their combat experiences than their fellow service men and women engaged in land battles. Perhaps air crews were more detached from the horrific outcomes of modern warfare, because they were thousands of feet above the carnage unfolding below them. These less personalised encounters may have resulted in fewer PTSD problems later emerging in post-war life.

14

GREAT ESCAPES

Generous acts of mateship performed by Warrant Officer Ernest (Ernie) Brough have already been documented in the previous chapter. Ernie was also awarded a Military Medal, (MM), for successfully undertaking a daring escape from a World War II German POW camp.

After leaving school at 13, Ernie Brough worked as an apprentice butcher in the Victorian town of Drouin, for which he was paid less than a dollar a week. He delivered meat to customers on horseback or bicycle. In his leisure time Ernie enjoyed shooting expeditions, playing football with the local club, and having a few beers with his young mates.

Ernie habitually 'likes to do the right thing', so when World War II broke out he succumbed to peer group pressure and volunteered for military service with many mates from his home area. Commitment to war service may also have been a part of his genetic make-up, as legendary World War I hero, Albert Jacka, was his mother's cousin.

Ernie was 19 when he sought information about 'joining up' in Melbourne, and he was told to walk around the block until he turned 20. After a brief stroll around city streets, Ernie Brough was accepted for military service on that same day.

He was drafted into the army on 28th March 1940. Ernie trained at a variety of places which included Dandenong, the

Caulfield and Flemington Race Courses, Balcombe Army Camp and Port Melbourne. Private Ernest Brough then sailed on a Dutch freighter to Fremantle on 15th September 1940, and following this month-long voyage, he was shipped to Ashkelon in southern Israel. Six months of monotonous training was then undertaken, before Ernie was assigned to the 2/32nd Battalion, which arrived in Tobruk on 3rd May 1941.

In the desert campaign he became accustomed to being under heavy enemy fire, and the strong desire to be 'there for your mates' became vital for the morale of all Diggers. Conditions in the Western Desert campaigns were atrocious. The searing heat of day was replaced by the freezing cold of night. There were no toilets, so dysentery swept through the group. Fleas were prevalent in the camp, dust storms would rage for up to three days, and solders were unable to wash their clothes for weeks on end.

On 30th July 1941 the situation became grimmer. After clashing with an officious officer, Private Brough was sent out on what he regarded as a suicide mission. A bullet wound to his buttocks resulted, and Ernie was forced to recuperate in hospitals at Tobruk, the Suez Canal and Tel Aviv.

The still underweight and combat-fatigued Ernest Brough became a Non-Commissioned Officer (NCO), on his return to Tobruk. There he was assigned to build fortifications in appalling conditions, which saw temperatures often hover around 50 degrees Celsius.

In April 1942 Ernie's group was sent to combat Rommel's German troops at El Alamein. One of his allocated tasks was the identification of Australian soldiers' corpses, which had been abandoned in the desert for days. By then a battle-hardened Ernie Brough was starting to feel detached from reality, and was seemingly not badly affected by the gruesome experience.

In late October the situation momentarily improved for the Diggers. Ernie's rescue of the wounded German has already been documented in this book, and on that same mission he captured six other enemy soldiers.

The allies' success ended abruptly on 31st October 1942. Ernie and several others were suddenly surrounded by German tanks, and they became POWs. Following the departure of their German captors, they were transported to Italian POW camps in Bengasi and later in Reggio Calabria.

There they basically existed on a starvation diet, but Ernie still vividly recalls a welcome act of kindness from a local woman. One day when the heavily guarded POWs trudged through a busy street, she presented the noticeably emaciated Ernie with an orange. Ernie gratefully accepted the unexpected gift, which he later divided into small equal segments to share with 11 other POW mates.

The prisoners soon undertook an eight-hour train transfer to Camp PG 57 near the village of Gruppignano. This large compound housed 3,000 prisoners and millions of lice. It was Ernie's home for the next seven months. Winter there was extremely harsh, and it was in that hellish frozen camp, that Ernie saw an innocent fellow prisoner needlessly shot dead by the unpredictable Italian camp commandant.

The 16th February 1943 was Ernie's 23rd birthday, so he indulged himself with a 'gourmet treat'. In the six weeks leading up to his birthday, Ernie hoarded cheeses which had arrived in his Red Cross parcels, so that he could gorge himself in style on his special day. During his monotonous confinement Ernie also made a suitcase from jam jars, he played chess, and he grew carrots.

In mid- 1943 Italy surrendered, and the Germans transferred the POWs to Stalag 18 A/Z at Spittal in southern Austria, where conditions were much better. There the prisoners procured a wireless, and spirits rose when they heard the tide of the war was turning against Germany.

It was around that time when Ernie, New Zealander Eric Batty, Western Australian Alan Barry and the German speaking Englishman Matthew Gibson, began to seriously formulate escape plans.

The group was able to join work parties outside the enclosure, which alerted them to important landmarks for their planned exit. They secretly obtained a map of Europe and a compass, and tentatively chose Easter 1944, (when a full moon would enhance visibility), for their freedom quest. Unfortunately Gibson withdrew from the attempt, so only three potential escapees filled their camouflaged clothes with stolen food, and began their risky night-time escape attempt on 8th February 1944. After crawling under the camp boundary wire, the group walked 15 miles south towards Slovenia and the Adriatic Sea, on their first night of liberty.

For the next two incredible months the three fugitives virtually lived like feral animals. The days were mostly spent hidden from public view in haystacks, ditches, storm water drains, under fallen leaves in forests, and amidst tall growing crops. They often slept close together heads against stomachs on hard grounds in freezing conditions, their clothes were frequently wet, and food supplies were so scarce that they sometimes ate raw cabbage stalks and canola still growing in fields.

The chances of re-capture were ever present. They were once bailed up by a fierce guard dog, they risked drowning when fast flowing and freezing streams needed to be crossed, and warming fires started by Alan's cigarette lighter probably saved them more than once from death by exposure. They also faced the possibility of being blown to bits from gunfire or hidden explosives, when they crawled under barbed wire fences.

A high degree of luck, and a few welcome acts of kindness from local farmers and partisan groups, helped the three escapees survive. At the time young Slovenian and Croatian men were being forcibly drafted into the German army. Often that resulted in them being sent to the dreaded Russian front, where casualties were high. Consequently some farmers, villagers and partisans were sympathetic toward foreigners on the run from the Gestapo. A few locals provided welcome meals for the trio, while others secretly left food supplies on gate posts.

Such generosity from anonymous well-wishers, boosted the morale of the desperate escapees, and 60 years on, Ernie still vividly recalls a particular evening, when he heard local women happily singing in harmony with each other. The sound of their tuneful voices drifting pleasantly through the calm evening air, reminded Ernie that people still indulged in harmless normal pleasures. He knew that similar enjoyments awaited him, when he was free and safe back in Australia.

On one occasion the trio shared the pleasures of warm mineral springs with a local group of men. The English speaking fugitives were careful not to speak a word to the curious locals, but fate decreed that the occasion would resurface at a future date. Twenty years later, in his home-city of Perth, Alan Barry was stopped in a city street by a Yugoslav migrant. He recognised Alan, and it soon became apparent that he shared that mineral bath with Alan, when the Western Australian escapee was evading his German enemies.

After two anxious months the fugitives reached the outskirts of Banja Luka in northern Bosnia, and on the 10th June 1944 partisans provided the welcome news that a United States plane was coming to rescue them and 28 other refugees.

The group helped put piles of wood along a primitive runway, but, in the foggy night-time conditions, the rescue plane overshot the runway and disappeared down the hill.

Next day the American pilot wished to burn the now bogged plane, but the desperate escapees refused to consider that suggestion. The three Anzacs, other war refugees, and their partisan friends cut down saplings for support slats after digging channels through the oozy mud. Early that afternoon, 40 bullocks miraculously appeared from somewhere. They were hitched to the aeroplane, which was then dragged safely through the mud to the runway on the hill.

After the aircraft's hydraulics was checked, 31 multi-cultural refugees were air lifted to Italy, where they were de-briefed in Naples. The three Anzacs then travelled by boat and plane to Cairo, and finally, on the 11th September 1944, Ernie arrived safely in Port Melbourne. There he was greeted by his happy and relieved parents, who had received scant news about their son's welfare during much of the war years. Soon after, Warrant Officer Ernest Brough was awarded a MM, for displaying 'courage in persistent attempts to escape from POW camps'.

Ernie Brough's Military Medal

Overall, his return to Australian civilian life was traumatic. During his initial six weeks of leave from the army, Ernie became an alcoholic 'tear-away', who would vanish for days but remember little of what had transpired. Well-meaning invitations for afternoon tea to homes in Drouin were rejected, because of the nervous shaking habit which Ernie developed in his left hand. He also found it difficult to return to his trade as a butcher.

He briefly became a war loans salesman, but it was in a Ballarat rehabilitation centre that Ernie Brough began to put his life back in order. There he began to take pride in making leather handbags. Working with his hands in a wholly predictable environment, proved to be therapeutic for a man who had lived with danger each day for months, and who treated every shadow as if it was a dangerous predator.

Irrational rages often consumed him, but Ernie became calmer and happier once Edna May Stevenson waltzed into his life. He first met her at a dance in Ballarat. The couple soon fell in love, and they were married on 4th August 1945.

Previously Ernie left the army, after declining to further his military career at an officer's school, but a stint at farming near Warragul proved unsatisfactory. Worrying bouts of PTSD were again being endured. However the birth of Gayle Narelle Brough, after seven years of marriage, brought more serenity to Ernie's life and he began managing a successful butcher's shop in Drouin.

He enjoyed re-uniting with Eric in New Zealand and Alan in Western Australia in the late 1990s, but both his escapee mates have since died. By 1999 Edna was starting to show signs of advancing dementia. Ernie gave up working as a part-time gardener to look after her in their Geelong home, but her health declined quickly after she broke her hip in a fall. Edna Brough was 81 when she died on 27th June 2004.

Ernie experienced many horrific incidents during World War II, but this humble hero has never lost his generosity or sense of decency. After selling a highly valued block of land near Geelong, Ernie Brough gifted half the proceeds to his daughter and granddaughter, while the sum remaining funded a valuable piece of life saving machinery in a Melbourne hospital. He is still quite content to live frugally on his war pension. The proceeds he received from sales of his fascinating autobiography *Dangerous Days- A Digger's Great Escape* have all been donated to Alzheimer research programs.

Ernie is now 94. He continues to live independently in his Belmont home, and this last surviving 'rat of Tobruk' from the Geelong area, still enjoys the comradeship of his Digger mates at the Geelong RSL.

*

Ian Busst now resides in Brighton's Anzac Hostel, which is a Melbourne based Veterans' and Widows' retirement home. He was 96 in October 2014, and this feisty warrior has led an eventful life. At the age of six he was struck down with infantile paralysis, and he left school when he was only 12. He commuted by bicycle to the city for his first job, for which he was paid one shilling a week.

In later years, Ian Busst became a POW for three years. During those 36 months none of his captors knew that he had recorded key events on his well concealed Leica camera.

After previously pulling a man clear from a burning truck, Ian Busst was often referred to as 'that mad old bugger'.

Remarkably, he escaped from POW camps on two occasions. The first breakout took place in northern Italy, and he also went under the wire from a Munich camp.

He was first captured in the Western Desert during World War II. Busst counted himself as unlucky on that occasion, as his German captor was effectively masquerading as a British officer. From Africa he was transferred to Camp 57 near Trieste Italy, where a fervent Fascist named Vittorio Calcaterra was his Camp Commandant. Busst endured 18 horrific months under this sadistic tyrant's rule, but the situation improved after he was transferred to a farm prison near Vercelli.

On 10th July 1943, 'that mad old buggar' and ten other inmates escaped, and headed towards neutral Switzerland. Local Italian partisans hid them from the pursuing Germans, but the POWs were unfortunately recaptured only a day away from a safe refuge.

As punishment, Ian Busst was sent to a Munich labour

camp in an area which was being heavily bombed by allied planes. Busst and other prisoners were assigned rescue missions of local civilians injured by allied air raids, and they witnessed many horrific sights. A disgruntled Polish guard helped Ian in his second POW escape, but 'that mad old bugger' returned secretly to the camp when it became clear that his whereabouts was known to the Germans.

Ian Busst returned to Australia five years, two months and 22 days after leaving our shores for the World War II battle front. This married man with three children spent ten years as a farmer, and he later worked as a truck driver and carpenter.

*

Australia, as a signatory nation to the Geneva Convention, has long held the belief that wartime POWs have the right to attempt escapes from enemy prison camps. Furthermore, if POWs are recaptured they should not be punished for their failed attempts.

During the Pacific War Japan did not adhere to the Geneva Convention charter, and its cruel treatment of captured POWs at the Selarang Barracks in Singapore was later viewed as being a crime against humanity.

On 30th October 1942, Commander General Shimpei Fukuye demanded that all prisoners sign a 'no escape pledge', after two British and two Australian POWs were apprehended shortly after they escaped from the compound. When the Commander's request was refused, the two most senior Australian POW officers were forced to witness the firing squad executions of fellow Australians, Corporal Rodney

Breavington and Private Victor Gale. Finally the POW chain of command reluctantly ordered all inmates to honour this pledge agreement, which became meaningless after many of the POWs signed their name as 'Ned Kelly'.

In 1946 military justice finally prevailed, for in the year after Japan surrendered, Fukuye, the then imprisoned former commandant of Selarang, was found guilty of committing crimes against humanity at a Singapore War Crimes trial. He was subsequently executed in exactly the same way as his two Australian victims.

*

Paul Royle, an Australian serving with the RAF in Europe during World War II, became a POW after his Bristol Blenheim Bomber was shot down by a German Luftwaffe fighter plane. The Western Australian elected to stay with his badly wounded navigator mate after landing in Germany, but was captured the following day.

At first Pilot Officer Royle was imprisoned at Stalag Luft 1 on the Baltic Sea, where he was arrested while building an escape tunnel. Royle was then sent to Stalag Luft 111 on the Polish border, from where it was considered impossible to escape.

Paul Royle was undeterred by the harsher environment, and became part of a 200 strong group which was determined to 'break-out'. British prisoner Roger Bushel, (dubbed 'Big X'), was the group's leader, and he planned for three tunnels to be dug, which were code-named 'Tom', 'Dick' and 'Harry'. Dirt dug up by the group was stored in the diggers' underwear, and discreetly dropped on the ground later during walks around the camp. Inmates were amused by the awkward gait of the dirt-laden walkers, and nicknamed them 'the penguins'. Other prisoners assisted their fellow POWs, by forging documents and tailoring disguises for their return to civilian life.

Tunnel 'Harry' became the designated exit from the camp, and the order of departures was decided by ballot. Paul Royle believes that he was designated number 57 in the order of tunnel exits. The break-out took place on 2ⁿᵈ March 1944 on an icy cold and moonless night. When Paul reached the end of tunnel 'Harry', he was well clear of the camp, but still short of the edge of the nearby forest. Paul and an Englishman named Humphries hid in the forest next day, but they were recaptured soon after. Only three of the Stalag Luft 111 escapees finally reached England.

Paul Royle was 98, when he celebrated the anniversary of his attempted escape with his wife and sons in a Perth nursing home.

A film titled *The Great Escape*, which was based on this event, was produced in 1963. Steve McQueen, James Garner and the late Richard Attenborough all had starring roles in the movie.

15

ON A STREET NEAR YOU

Perhaps you sometimes wonder, when you see older people in your local shopping centre, what major events have occurred in their lives.

There is every possibility that they experienced war service, or they know others of similar vintage who are war veterans. The profiles in this chapter provide snapshots of wartime service. Some commitments were brief and relatively stress free, but they still have similarities to other war service involvements across Australia.

*

Doctor Bruce Jones is now 94, and he resides at the Drysdale Grove Aged Care facility in Victoria. He was a local doctor in various parts of Australia, until he elected to practice on the Bellarine Peninsula, where he later retired.

His parents were both teachers, and Bruce had commenced a medical degree at Melbourne

University when World War II began. Various influences including patriotism, peer group pressure and the opportunity for new adventures stimulated Bruce's ambitions to train with the Australian Air Force.

Initially he was a 'Choco'- a conscripted soldier, who was

assigned duties with the 20th Field Ambulance Corps, where he became a stretcher bearer and a NCO.

After undergoing basic training, Bruce Jones fortunately received his Air Force call-up. Over the next few months he undertook specialised training in air gunnery and wireless navigation at Somers, Ballarat, West Sale and Mt. Gambier. He then travelled by train to Perth, after graduating as a Navigator Wireless Operator, (Navigator W). Various postings then eventuated around the country, until Bruce commenced a specialist course on Wackett single engine aeroplanes at Ballarat. By that stage of preparation only 25% of students progressed to pilot training programs. Bruce recalls one new graduate being summarily demoted following his low-flying debut flight, after he 'buzzed' the Ballarat-Geelong passenger train.

Bruce then returned to West Sale for experience with Fairy Battle planes. These aircrafts were commonly called 'flying coffins', because of their high casualty rate. The number of fatalities was particularly noticeable among inexperienced airmen, with 27% of deaths occurring during training, while 33% were KIA on their first tour of duty.

Bruce Jones commenced war duties in the Banda Sea area close to Darwin. He served in a two man crew. Clive Terdich from Melbourne was usually his pilot and bomb aimer, while Bruce attended to navigational needs.

In early missions a faulty escape hatch caused much anxiety, especially when it unexpectedly opened 30,000 feet above the Pacific Ocean. In their low level bombing raids Clive and Bruce attacked Japanese shipyards, roads and seaways. They were fortunately not subjected to aerial combats.

His most hazardous mission occurred shortly before

the Australians invaded Borneo. They had targeted the Japanese base of Menado, which was approached over a steep escarpment. Heavy enemy fire was encountered, and many inaccurate anti-aircraft shells produced water spouts in the ocean below, before the mission was successfully accomplished.

After the war ended Bruce became involved in the evacuation of POWs, mostly from the notorious island of Ambon, a well- known wartime 'hell-hole' in present day Indonesia. An estimated 70% of interned POWs perished there.

After enjoying a more relaxed assignment in post-war Japan, Bruce Jones resumed his medical training at Melbourne University, from where he graduated in 1950. In retrospect, he would not change the course of his long life, and Bruce Jones still enjoys the fellowship of other war veterans at the Drysdale Sub Branch of the RSL.

*

Geoffrey Wisley was the only son of a family of three, born to Frederick ('Ted') and Annie ('Fairy') Wisley on 19th November 1923. He attended State Schools in South Geelong and Drysdale, and returned to school to obtain his Merit Certificate, after first leaving at the age of 13. Geoff then worked as an agricultural labourer and grocery assistant, until he was called-up for World War II military service.

He undertook basic training at Bonegilla, Watsonia and Werribee, where he was assigned to the 112 Ack-Ack Anti-Aircraft Unit as a gunner. On 15th September 1942, Geoff's Battery departed from Dandenong, and slowly made their way by road to Darwin, where they were stationed at Bachelor Airport. There they were subjected to bombing attacks from low flying Japanese aircraft, and it was later reported that Geoff's ground crew recorded a 'hit' on an enemy plane, which subsequently plunged into the ocean.

Authorities allegedly reported that only 12 local people perished in air raids over Darwin, but it was rumoured among the troops stationed there, that hundreds of body bags were distributed after attacks. None of them returned empty.

Geoff was later transferred by boat to the Philippines, where he worked with the International Red Cross, which was returning POWs to their home countries. While working in Manilla Geoff met Lady Mountbatten, and her friendly and charming manner left a lasting impression on the young Australian.

Geoff was married after returning home, but 16 days later he was transferred to New Guinea to guard Japanese prisoners. Finally, after recording 30 months of war service in tropical areas of the Pacific, Geoffrey Wisley was discharged from the army on 28th June 1948.

Most of his working life was then spent in Geelong, where Geoff Wisley became a senior supervisor with International Harvester and later the Ford Motor Company, before retiring from the work force in 1983. Since then he has been an active golfer, and this energetic 91-year-old has served as President of the Drysdale Sub-Branch of the RSL for at least 15 years.

*

Francis ('Frank') Ambrose Pickett was born in 1925 in Coleraine, a town in the south-west of Victoria. He was the seventh born of nine children, and his father, William James Pickett, owned a mixed farm. Frank's mother Rose died when he was only six, and he and his brother Lawrence stayed with their grandmother in Brighton for six months, while their father coped with his changed situation.

After returning Frank walked two miles each week day to attend the local Catholic school in Coleraine, but the needs of the family farm meant that his school based education ended when he was 13.

Life on the farm was arduous. Frank would often help his father plant over 100 acres of crops, and four siblings and he hand-milked a dozen cows twice a day. Even when he was still a schoolboy, Frank was responsible for providing kindling each day for household fires. These long hours of work prohibited any involvement in local sport, but occasionally home-based boxing matches were organised with other local farming families.

The advent of World War II completely changed their status quo. Five of the boys enlisted, (and thankfully all of them returned from the war), while the two sisters found employment in a Melbourne munitions factory. In early September 1943, 18-year-old Frank followed his brother Lawrence into the RAAF, and he was posted to Shepparton for two months of basic training.

It was a 'hard slog'. After lacing up his new boots, Frank and his fellow rookies tackled an 11 mile march, which made walking a difficult exercise for the next three days. During one of their over-night camping assignments, Frank and his tent mates were joined by a tiger snake, while six others were discovered in the thatched roofs of their quarters!

After providing maintenance for Air Force flying boats

at Lake Boga, Frank was posted first to Bradfield Park near Sydney, and then to Townsville with the 109 Fighter Control Unit. A fortnight later the unit travelled to New Guinea, where aircraft maintenance duties continued at the Jackson Strip airport near Port Moresby. Fortunately, during their two months of service, they were not subjected to enemy bombing raids.

Frank's most frightening wartime experiences occurred in the air. His group flew perilously close to mountains on the Owen Stanley Ranges, when they were transferred to the Nazab 42 Operational Base Unit in the Markham Valley. There they serviced and loaded bombs into US Liberator aeroplanes.

At nearby Dobadura, torrential rain caused the creek 15 feet below them to suddenly flood their quarters. Fortunately Frank was in Port Moresby Hospital receiving attention to a badly injured leg, when another flood swept away his former Dobadura quarters. Three Australian servicemen drowned in that accident.

A second traumatic flight took place on the way home by flying boat, which developed engine troubles and flew dangerously close to sugar cane fields near Bundaberg. Fortunately the pilot made a perfect landing on the nearby Burnett River. A four-day train trip was then undertaken before Frank received further attention to his leg at the Heidelberg Repatriation Hospital.

Previously, when Frank was in New Guinea, his father had sold the Coleraine farm and had relocated to Geelong. Frank moved to that area and worked with T.W. Jewel's Cabinet Makers after completing a six-month course. He then operated his own carrying business for three years, he purchased and operated a mixed grocery store in Chilwell for some time, and for the next 47 years he became a successful real estate agent in Belmont, Leopold and Geelong.

During those years Frank became a prominent local sportsman. He displayed considerable skill in cricket, golf, tennis and snooker, and the now 89-year-old remains a champion lawn bowler, despite coping with at least six operations to his hip, leg and toes.

Frank married June in 1950, and their union produced a daughter and a son, before June died in 2004. Frank later met a widow named Trish at the Clifton Springs Bowling Club, and the couple are now happily married.

Today Frank Pickett regards all wars as being a waste of lives and time. He has never returned to New Guinea or attended reunions with his former colleagues, though he is usually present at Anzac Day services at either Drysdale or Portland, where a 92-year-old sister resides.

*

Francis ('Frank') Alexander McLennan was born at the Melbourne suburb of Newport in 1926. He was John McLennan's only son, and the youngest of three children. Frank's mother, Millicent, died when he was only 12.

John McLennan was a World War I veteran, who was initially discharged with a broken leg while serving in Egypt. After recovering, he enlisted again and saw action as a tunneller in Belgium on the Western Front. In this highly dangerous role, John's group was once so close to the enemy that they overheard their conversations, while they were setting up explosives in a nearby tunnel.

Sir John Monash was his commanding officer, and John McLennan greatly respected the renowned General's leadership skills. Frank was five when Monash died in 1931, and his father and he joined thousands of others at the great man's Melbourne funeral parade.

Frank received his formal education at the North Williamstown State School and the Footscray Technical College, before he began work as a boiler maker.

After World War II broke out Frank volunteered to be an air force gunner, but was unsuccessful because his employer would not release the 18-year-old from his job. Frank, who was motivated by his spirit of adventure and his father's previous example, persisted in his efforts. Finally in 1945 he successfully volunteered for military service, even though World War II hostilities had ceased.

Frank A. McLennan received his army training at Greta, Ingleburn and Rooty Hill in NSW, and was then transferred to Broadmeadows in Victoria for six months. He was allowed to commute to the army camp there from his Newport home, but still did his share of guard duty stints at the Broadmeadows base.

During his training period Frank A. McLennan was called upon to repair a wheelchair, which had been broken by his cousin, Frank D. McLennan. The two had become close friends, after spending many happy holidays together at Frank D's home in Wodonga.

Frank D. had served in New Guinea, where he was awarded a Military Medal (MM) but he had received a shot in the groin from a Japanese sniper. He was recovering back in Australia, when he and two rowdy pub companions all attempted to hitch a ride on the same wheelchair. Ambulance officers attended to their minor injuries, but it took the specialised skills of Frank A. McLennan to restore the wheelchair's health.

Frank D. McLennan

After being kitted out in three army uniforms, Frank A. McLennan's unit boarded the 'Manoora' at Sydney in the early months of 1947, and commenced the long voyage to Japan. At Rabaul and various South Sea islands they collected approximately 80 Japanese ex-soldiers, who were housed in separate decks. After being de-loused, the largely unwanted Japanese travellers were released in Hiroshima, where apparently no relatives or friends were there to greet them.

Frank's Battalion was attached to the British Commonwealth Occupational Forces (BCOF), which was stationed at Kure, where many sunken ships were visible in the bay. There Frank and a mechanically trained sergeant were responsible for testing army jeeps, staff cars and trucks. Leave was granted after nine months of duty, and he learned to ski in the colder southern part of the country.

Frank wished to remain with the BCOF, and if his hopes had been met, he would probably have served in Korea, where war broke out in 1950. Instead, he was discharged after returning to Australia. He then returned to his Newport job and married Betty in 1948. Their nearly seventy years of marriage have now produced two children, two grandchildren and six great grandchildren.

Over the years the Frank A. McLennan family resided in the Victorian Otway Ranges town of Weeaproinah, where

Frank worked in the timber industry, until he was struck down with rheumatic fever. They also lived in Spotswood, until moving permanently to Clifton Springs in 1986. For over 20 years Frank A. McLennan enjoyed lawn bowls at the local club. He still keeps in touch with his army mates, and has attended many reunions over the years.

John Ramsay Williams was born on 1st February 1926. John spent his early years in the Dandenong Ranges town of Olinda, before moving to Surrey Hills. When he was 15, his mother and sisters returned to Olinda, but John remained in Surrey Hills and was domiciled with a friend's parents.

He left school after obtaining his Merit Certificate, and started work with the Wemberly Engineering and Refrigeration Company. John enjoyed his leisure time with the Air Force cadets, and when he was 18 he enlisted for military service with the Air Force on 11th February 1944.

His initial army training was spent at the Box Hill Technical College, where he received instruction in Morse code and other related issues. A three-month stint in Adelaide followed, before John moved to the Melbourne Showgrounds, where living conditions were very basic. There he became an expert in Spitfire engines.

John was then transferred to West Sale airport where he gained experience at the Air Gunnery School. He remained at Sale until he was discharged from the military services on 4th September 1946. Overall, he regards his late call-up into military service as a positive experience.

Back in civilian life, John Williams completed a Fitting and Turning course at Swinburne Technical College, and he and his wife June raised a family of four sons and a daughter. He worked in various areas, including Morwell where he was employed as a pipe fitter in the then emerging brown coal industry.

The final 13 years of his working life were spent with the Gadstone Can Company, where he was a mechanical fitter. He retired to Clifton Springs in 1990, and the now widowed John Williams devotes his time to his extensive and well maintained garden, to his activities at the local Probus Club, and to many enjoyable times at the Clifton Springs Bowling Club.

Frank Pickett

Frank A McLennan

John Williams

BIBLIOGRAPHY

Age newspaper (May 2014- April 2015)

Australian War Memorial Library

Bomber Command 2012 Commemorative Mission Program

Brough, Ernest J. *Dangerous Days-A Digger's Great Escape.* Harper Collins, Sydney NSW 2009.

Clark, Neville 'Boz' *Aviator Farmer Schoolmaster W.R.* Parsons Publisher, Ocean Grove Victoria 2010

DJ & M Desktop Publishing, Queensland *A History of the Members of 87TPTPLRAASG* 2012

Ferguson, Ian *Aussie War Heroes* Brolga Publishing Pty Ltd 2012

Ferguson, Ian *Disasters That Shocked Australia* Brolga Publishing Pty Ltd 2009

FitzSimons, Peter *Kokoda* Hodder Headline group, NSW 2004

Gammage, Bill *The Broken Years* Penguin Books Australia 1974

Hamilton, John *The Price of Valour* Pan McMillan Australia 2012

Hill, Anthony *Soldier Boy* Penguin Books Australia 2001

History of the Second World War (collection of monthly magazines)

Hunter-Payne, Gwynedd *On the Duckboards* Allen & Unwin Pty Ltd Australia 1995

Kraznoth, Stanley *Where to for Valour?* Shale Press 1995

Ramage ,Gary & McPhedran, Ian *Afghanistan: Australia's War* Harper Collins Publishers, 2014.

RSL News Queensland 2014

Sunday Age Newspaper (May 2014--April 2015)

Wikipedia- The Free Encyclopedia www.wikipedia.com

WARS THAT NEVER END

Ian Ferguson

ISBN 9781922175823		Qty
RRP	AU$24.99	.....
Postage within Australia	AU$5.00	.....
	TOTAL* $_____	
	* All prices include GST	

Name:..

Address: ....

....

Phone:...

Email: ....

Payment: ❑ Money Order ❑ Cheque ❑ MasterCard ❑Visa

Cardholder's Name:..

Credit Card Number: ....

Signature:...

Expiry Date: ....

Allow 7 days for delivery.

Payment to: Marzocco Consultancy (ABN 14 067 257 390)
    PO Box 12544
    A'Beckett Street, Melbourne, 8006
    Victoria, Australia
    admin@brolgapublishing.com.au

BE PUBLISHED

Publish through a successful publisher.
Brolga Publishing is represented through:
• **National** book trade distribution, including sales,
marketing & distribution through **Macmillan Australia.**
• **International** book trade distribution to
  • The United Kingdom
  • North America
  • Sales representation in South East Asia
• **Worldwide** e-Book distribution

For details and inquiries, contact:
Brolga Publishing Pty Ltd
PO Box 12544
A'Beckett St VIC 8006

Phone: 0414 608 494
markzocchi@brolgapublishing.com.au
ABN: 46 063 962 443
(Email for a catalogue request)